MEET THE REAL JESUS

EXPLORE EYEWITNESS ACOUNTS
IN 40 BITE-SIZED PIECES

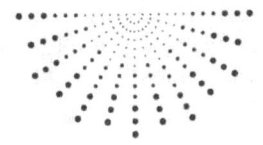

BELINDA POLLARD

Copyright © Belinda Pollard 2022, belindapollard.com.

Small Blue Dog Publishing, PO Box 310, Lawnton Queensland 4501, Australia. smallbluedog.com – ask@smallbluedog.com

This text is revised and rewritten from the text of *Closer to God for Newcomers: Meet the Real Jesus* © Belinda Pollard, first published by Scripture Union 2001 and reprinted with revisions 2005, 2010.

Edition 2

ISBN

Paperback: 978-0-6482672-7-0

Ebook: 978-0-6482672-8-7

All rights reserved. No part of this book may be reproduced in any form or by any electronic or mechanical means, including information storage and retrieval systems, without written permission from the author, except for the use of brief quotations in a book review.

Scripture quotations marked (NIV) taken from The Holy Bible, New International Version® NIV® Copyright © 1973, 1978, 1984, 2011 by Biblica, Inc. Used with permission. All rights reserved worldwide.

Scripture quotations marked (WEB) are from the World English Bible which is in the public domain.

Cover image via Bigstock copyright © benicce

Author image copyright © Tania Jovanovic

 Created with Vellum

For Mum:
Thank you for urging me to republish this book,
and for helping me to meet the real Jesus.

WHO ON EARTH IS JESUS CHRIST?

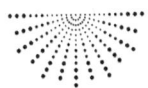

Twenty-one centuries after His sandals scuffed the dusty roads of Palestine, Jesus Christ is still a household name. How many other 2000-year-old people are still influential?

If you live in the western world, you might think Christianity is on the way out. Attendance at church services is falling, and the Christian world view is increasingly absent from popular culture. I meet people who use "Jesus" as a swearword without knowing what it means.

But hang on a minute…

In Africa and Asia, Christianity is exploding. One in four Christians in the world today lives in Africa. There are churches in South Korea with hundreds of thousands of members. China was home to only 5000 Christians in the 1960s, but, according to various sources, has between 44 million and 130 million today.

The picture is more complex than it might at first appear.

DO YOU WONDER?

Are you curious about a man who could have such an enduring impact on the world? Maybe you are skeptical, but you want to be sure before you dismiss Christianity. Maybe you are a Seeker of Truth, thirsty for meaning in your life, and exploring many options. Maybe you can't stop wondering if Jesus is different to all the other gurus.

Maybe you have heard some good things about Jesus but have found the actions of His followers confusing and even repellent.

Maybe you are a new believer or a long-time Christian who wants to refresh their connection with Jesus.

WHERE CAN WE FIND THE TRUTH ABOUT JESUS?

No respected secular historian disputes the existence of Jesus of Nazareth, although they might have different understandings of his role.

As a student journalist many years ago, I was taught to get as close to the source of an event as possible. That's why in this book I am going to focus on eyewitness accounts of the life of Jesus that have been published in the Christian Bible. I believe they will take us as close as we can get to the air Jesus breathed, the texture of the dust between His toes, and the events that moved Him to compassion, anger and loving sacrifice.

If we can find the What, Where, Why and How, perhaps we can understand the Who.

OUR SOURCE

There are four "authorized biographies" or life stories of Jesus in the Bible, each one named for its author: Matthew, Mark, Luke, and John.

These are living, breathing accounts, full of conflict and compassion, great courage and narrow escapes, and a hope that emerges from the midst of tragedy.

Matthew wrote with a theme of showing how Jesus fulfills many centuries of Jewish prophecy. Mark feels like the news journalist of the group to me – his account is short and snappy, no filler. John is poetic and philosophical.

In this book we will focus on the gospel (good news) written by a man named Luke, a doctor by profession who researched and compiled eyewitness accounts of Jesus' life. Choosing Luke also allows us to go a few years further because he went on to write about the early Christian church in the decades after Jesus' death.

WHAT IS THE BIBLE?

The Bible is actually a library of 66 books by different authors from various backgrounds, written over more than a thousand years, all building the truth about Jesus.

The Bible was originally written in ancient languages including Hebrew, first-century Greek, and Aramaic. There are a variety of English translations, including the King James Version (KJV) that many people have heard snippets of. The KJV dates back to the 17th Century and has a beautiful Shakespearean feel to the language.

When you see letters such as NIV or WEB after a Bible quotation in this book, they refer to different translations – in this case the New International Version (NIV) and the World English Bible (WEB).

We are using modern translations in this book to make it easier to grasp the meaning quickly.

You can buy a printed or ebook Bible in bookstores, borrow it from libraries, read it online at sites like biblegateway.com or in apps on your phone or tablet, or listen to it as an audiobook.

WHAT DO THE NUMBERS MEAN?

The numbers you see marked in Bible texts and which are reproduced in this book are divisions added in the Middle Ages to make it easier for us to discuss particular segments together.

- A large number is a chapter.
- Small, superscript numbers which appear every sentence or two are verses.
- They are referred to like this: Luke 1:10, where the book is called Luke, and we are focusing on the first chapter, and the tenth verse of that first chapter.
- To suggest you look at a particular verse, I might say "as mentioned in verse 10" or after a comment add (verse 10), so that you can check it out for yourself.

HOW TO GET THE MOST OUT OF THIS BOOK

This book contains forty short chapters designed so that, if you wish, you can read one a day. That allows thinking time as you explore the story of Jesus over a few weeks.

Each chapter includes a short piece of the Bible,

followed by an exploration of some of the terms and historical setting, plus thought starters for why it matters. It also includes a snippet from elsewhere in the Bible, showing how the whole message hangs together.

AN INVITATION

I invite you to come to the life of Jesus with an open mind and a receptive heart. If you feel inadequate, uncertain, or skeptical, you might like to say (aloud or silently in your head) before each chapter: God, if you exist, show me the truth of Jesus Christ, and show me why it matters.

1
SURPRISING NEWS FOR A YOUNG WOMAN – AND US

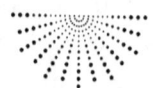

You are about to embark on a journey into God's message to you. Ask God to help you understand what He will say to you today and in the coming weeks. You could say out loud or silently in your head: "God, if you exist, show me the truth of Jesus Christ, and show me why it matters."

READ LUKE 1:26–38 (WEB)

²⁶ Now in the sixth month, the angel Gabriel was sent from God to a city of Galilee named Nazareth, ²⁷ to a virgin pledged to be married to a man whose name was Joseph, of the house of David. The virgin's name was Mary. ²⁸ The angel went to her and said, "Greetings, you highly favored one! The Lord is with you."

²⁹ But when she saw him, she was greatly troubled at the saying, and considered what kind of greeting this might be. ³⁰ The angel said to her, "Don't be afraid, Mary, for you have found favor with God. ³¹ Behold, you will conceive in your womb and give birth to a son, and shall name him Jesus. ³² He will be great and will be

called the Son of the Most High. The Lord God will give him the throne of his father David, **33** and he will reign over Jacob's descendants forever, and of his kingdom there will be no end."

34 Mary said to the angel, "How can this be, since I am a virgin?"

35 The angel answered her, "The Holy Spirit will come on you, and the power of the Most High will overshadow you. Therefore also the holy one who is born from you will be called the Son of God. **36** Behold, Elizabeth your relative also has conceived a son in her old age; and this is the sixth month with her who was called barren. **37** For nothing spoken by God is impossible."

38 Mary said, "Behold, I am the servant of the Lord; let it be to me according to your word."

Then the angel departed from her.

EXPLORE

Our world abounds with stories of unusual births. Surrogates and grandmothers are having babies. IVF has become common. I knew a woman who, like Mary's elderly cousin Elizabeth (verse 36), was declared infertile by her doctors, only to become suddenly and astonishingly pregnant some years later.

However, only one child in the history of the planet was ever conceived without any contribution from a human father. His name is Jesus (which means "God is salvation"), and He is a descendant of the royal line of the ancient Jewish king, David (verse 32).

Since David's reign ended, the Jewish people had waited nearly a thousand years for the promised new king who would rule like him. They were hoping for someone to release them from Roman oppression, but

Jesus would be much more – He would rule eternally (verse 33).

The virgin birth is the proof of Jesus' parentage. His mother was a young Jewish girl named Mary, and His Father was the all-powerful God (verse 35).

If there is anything about Christianity that you find hard to accept (including the virgin birth!), don't be afraid to ask God honest questions. Mary asked the angel for more information (verse 34), and then chose to believe (verse 38). Ask God to help you understand. He is interested in you and will hear you.

ELSEWHERE IN THE BIBLE

700 years in advance, a Jewish prophet predicted Jesus' unusual birth.

> Therefore the Lord himself will give you a sign: The virgin will conceive and give birth to a son, and will call him Immanuel [which means: "God with us"].

— ISAIAH 7:14 (NIV)

2
CHRISTMAS

At least one third of the earth's population celebrate Christmas. Someone told someone else who told someone else... and finally even you and I heard about the birth of Jesus.

You might like to read the following Bible quote as though you have never heard of Christmas. What new things do you notice?

READ LUKE 2:1–14 (WEB)

¹ Now in those days, a decree went out from Caesar Augustus that all the world should be registered. ² This was the first registration [census] made when Quirinius was governor of Syria. ³ All went to be registered, everyone to his own town.

⁴ Joseph also went up from Galilee, out of the city of Nazareth, into Judea, to David's city, which is called Bethlehem, because he was of the house and line of David; ⁵ to be registered with Mary, who was pledged to be married to him, and was expecting a child.

⁶ While they were there, the day came for her to give

birth. ⁷ She gave birth to her firstborn son. She wrapped him in swaddling cloths, and laid him in a manger, because there was no room for them in the inn.

⁸ There were shepherds in the same region out in the field, and keeping watch over their flock by night. ⁹ Behold, an angel of the Lord appeared to them, and the glory of the Lord shone around them, and they were terrified. ¹⁰ The angel said to them, "Don't be afraid, for behold, I bring you good news of great joy which will be for all the people. ¹¹ For there is born to you today, in David's city, a Savior, who is Christ the Lord. ¹² This will be the sign to you: you will find a baby wrapped in swaddling cloths and lying in a feeding trough."

¹³ Suddenly, there was with the angel a multitude of the heavenly army praising God, and saying,

¹⁴ "Glory to God in the highest, and on earth peace among those on whom his favor rests."

EXPLORE

Christmas can be a magical time for both adults and children. In my city, Santa's Workshops appear in department stores while familiar carols serenade us. It can be easy to think it is all a pleasant seasonal fairytale.

But Luke reports angels (verses 9,13), shepherds (verse 8) and the baby in the feedbox (verse 7) in almost the same breath as a census decreed by a specific Roman Caesar (verse 1), when a specific governor was in power (verse 2). The baby away in a manger, the heavenly choir and the terrified shepherds are all anchored in time. In a small town in a quiet corner of the mighty Roman Empire, Jesus of Nazareth was born.

This is no fairytale. This is history.

Jesus' birth turns the world upside down. The all-powerful Savior of the world enters human life as a helpless baby. The great King from the royal line of David is born to poor parents, not in a palace but in an animal shelter. The birth announcement is made not to world rulers or people of influence but to simple shepherds (verse 9).

"Heavenly host" (verse 13) is a military term, but the most terrifying army in the universe comes proclaiming not war but peace (verse 14).

Jesus' method of entry ignores everything our world values — wealth, power, privilege. It is as though heaven has burst into earthly life with the birth of this child, challenging our priorities.

The angel's "good news of great joy" is for you too. God values you. Jesus was born to save you.

ELSEWHERE IN THE BIBLE

Another ancient prediction:

> For to us a child is born, to us a son is given, and the government will be on his shoulders. And he will be called Wonderful Counselor, Mighty God, Everlasting Father, Prince of Peace.
>
> — ISAIAH 9:6 (NIV)

3
THE ONE WHO FULFILLS ANCIENT PROMISES

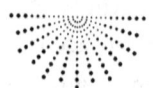

We live in a world of unkept promises. Marriages don't last "till death do us part," face creams don't remove wrinkles, jobs fall through, politicians change sides. It can make it hard for us to trust anyone or anything. Can you trust God? Ask Him to show you.

READ LUKE 2:25–35 (WEB)

25 Now, there was a man in Jerusalem whose name was Simeon. This man was righteous and devout, waiting for the consolation of Israel, and the Holy Spirit was on him. **26** It had been revealed to him by the Holy Spirit that he would not see death before he had seen the Lord's Christ. **27** He came in the Spirit into the temple. When the parents brought in the child, Jesus, to do for him according to the custom of the Law, **28** he took him into his arms, and blessed God, and said,

29 "Lord, now you are releasing your servant in peace according to your word; **30** for my eyes have seen your salvation, **31** which you have prepared in the presence of all peoples; **32** a light for revelation to the nations, and the glory of your people Israel."

33 The child's father and his mother were marveling at the things which were spoken about him, **34** and Simeon blessed them, and said to Mary, his mother, "Behold, this child is destined to cause the falling and the rising of many in Israel, and for a sign which is spoken against, **35** that the thoughts of many hearts may be revealed. A sword will pierce through your own soul, also."

EXPLORE

When God became a human being, it wasn't a snap decision. God had been planning the rescue of the human race ever since the first humans rejected Him and tried to run the world their own way (see Genesis 3). He could have abandoned us, but instead He came after us, driven by His great love for us.

God's rescue plan involved one particular nation, the Jews. Over the course of perhaps 2000 years, He made promises to them about their role in bringing people from all nations to Himself (verse 32).

All these promises were fulfilled in one very special Jew, Jesus (verse 30). With the help of a revelation from God, Simeon recognized in the tiny baby Jesus everything righteous Jews had been waiting for (verses 25–27).

Jesus was a real person, born into a devout Jewish family (verse 27). The other people we meet in the pages of the Bible are just as real. I wonder how the new mother would have felt to hear such wonderful but also such tragic news about her son (verses 34–35). Simeon was bursting with the excitement of seeing all his hopes and expectations fulfilled. He could die happy (verses 26,29) now that he had seen what his people had been longing for.

Have you ever been hurt by someone's failure to keep a promise? God keeps His promises.

ELSEWHERE IN THE BIBLE

Jesus was the answer to a promise God made about 2000 years earlier to a man named Abraham, the first Jew.

> "I will make you into a great nation, and I will bless you; I will make your name great, and you will be a blessing. I will bless those who bless you, and whoever curses you I will curse; and all peoples on earth will be blessed through you."
>
> — GENESIS 12:2–3 (NIV)

4
REPENTANCE: TURNING AWAY AND TURNING TOWARDS

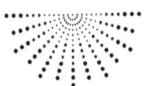

How do you react when people say you've done something wrong? I usually feel awkward and embarrassed and a bit defensive at first if they are right. However, a teachable heart is a great blessing. Consider what God's perspective might be.

READ LUKE 3:15-22 (WEB)

John, the son of Mary's elderly cousin Elizabeth, was out in the desert calling people to turn from their wickedness and be baptized – symbolically washed in the river. **15** As the people were in expectation, and all men were questioning in their hearts concerning John, whether perhaps he was the Christ, **16** John answered them all, "I baptize you with water, but one who is mightier than I is coming, the strap of whose sandals I am not worthy to untie. He will baptize you with the Holy Spirit and fire. **17** His winnowing fork is in his hand, to clear his threshing floor, and to gather the wheat into his barn; but he will burn up the chaff with unquenchable fire."

18 Then with many other exhortations he preached

good news to the people. ⁱ⁹ But Herod the tetrarch, being reproved by him for Herodias, his brother's wife, and for all the evil things Herod had done, ²⁰ added this to them all, that he locked up John in prison.

²¹ Now when all the people were baptized, Jesus also had been baptized, and was praying. The heavens were opened, ²² and the Holy Spirit descended on him in bodily form like a dove; and a voice came from heaven, saying, "You are my beloved Son. With you I am well pleased."

EXPLORE

The last of the Jewish prophets is ready to announce the Messiah's arrival. John the Baptist was a fiery preacher who didn't mind who he offended, even the adulterous king (verses 19–20). His outspokenness would eventually cost him his life, beheaded at Herod's command.

In contrast, ordinary people responded in droves to John's message, stricken by the news that they were on the wrong track, and eager to turn back to God.

As for the rumors that John might be the expected deliverer, his dismissive response is basically: "You ain't seen nothing yet" (verses 15–16).

Enter Jesus, and heaven bursts open on this dearly loved Son of God (verse 22). God pours himself into Jesus to empower Him for the three tough years of ministry that lie ahead (verse 22).

John points forward to an unpopular part of Jesus' job: judgement. The burning of chaff with unquenchable fire (verse 17) hardly sounds like "good news" (verse 18), but when you think about it, the destruction of evil and everything that hurts people *is* good news.

Baptism was a traditional Jewish way of showing a

change of heart (repentance). Jesus commanded His followers to be baptized as an outward sign that their lives have turned around and they now belong to Him.

"Repentance" is a permanent part of the Christian life. Even once we've made the big turnaround to follow Jesus, He will nudge us to smaller changes in direction our whole life long. If you feel as though Jesus wants you to turn away from something in your life, you can ask Him to give you the strength to do it.

ELSEWHERE IN THE BIBLE

> Therefore, I urge you, brothers and sisters, in view of God's mercy, to offer your bodies as a living sacrifice, holy and pleasing to God —this is your true and proper worship. Do not conform to the pattern of this world, but be transformed by the renewing of your mind. Then you will be able to test and approve what God's will is—his good, pleasing and perfect will.
>
> — ROMANS 12:1–2 (NIV)

5

THE PAIN OF TEMPTATION

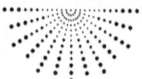

"I can resist everything except temptation," said Oscar Wilde, but it's really no laughing matter. We can hurt ourselves and others by giving in to small and large temptations, from eating too much junk food to having an affair with our best friend's spouse. Our relationship with God also suffers. Jesus knew the pain of temptation, but He also shows us a way forward.

READ LUKE 4:1–13 (WEB)

¹ Jesus, full of the Holy Spirit, returned from the Jordan, and was led by the Spirit into the wilderness ² for forty days, being tempted by the devil. He ate nothing during those days. Afterward, when they were ended, he was hungry. ³ The devil said to him, "If you are the Son of God, command this stone to become bread."

⁴ Jesus answered him, saying, "It is written, 'Man shall not live by bread alone.'"

⁵ The devil, leading him up on a high mountain, showed him all the kingdoms of the world in a moment of time. ⁶ The devil said to him, "I will give you all this

authority, and their glory, for it has been delivered to me; and I will give it to whomever I want. ⁷ If you therefore will worship me, it will all be yours."

⁸ Jesus answered him, "It is written, 'You shall worship the Lord your God, and you shall serve him only.'"

⁹ He led him to Jerusalem, and set him on the pinnacle of the temple, and said to him, "If you are the Son of God, throw yourself down from here, ¹⁰ for it is written, 'He will command his angels concerning you, to guard you;' ¹¹ and, 'On their hands they will bear you up, lest you strike your foot against a stone.'"

¹² Jesus answered him, "It is said, 'You shall not put the Lord your God to the test.'"

¹³ When the devil had completed every temptation, he departed from him until an opportune time.

EXPLORE

Out in the harsh Middle Eastern desert, after nearly six weeks without food (verse 2), Jesus shows us the strength of His character. The devil's suggestion (verse 3) sounds reasonable, but it is asking Jesus to use His power for His own benefit, a frequent temptation for those in leadership.

Jesus rejects the temptation by quoting the Bible (verse 4): "man does not live on bread alone but on every word that comes from the mouth of the Lord" (Deuteronomy 8:3). A free and open relationship with God is more nourishing even than food.

The second temptation is about power. The oppressive power of the day, the Roman Empire, was certainly on the devil's side, as are many of today's world governments (verse 6). It must have been tempting for Jesus to see an opportunity to stop the oppression of His own people (verse 7), but He recognized that whatever the appearances, God was ultimately in charge (verse 8).

The devil tries one last time, tempting Jesus to get God to prove himself (verse 9). This time even the devil quotes the Bible (verses 10–11)! But Jesus knows that to test God's promises in such a brazen way would be ultimately to say He didn't trust God (verse 12).

In the end, Jesus refuses to be drawn to spectacular, self-serving or short-term answers. He is determinedly devoted to God's eternal purposes.

If you are struggling with temptation, you can ask Jesus to help you – He came because it is impossible for us to be perfect.

ELSEWHERE IN THE BIBLE

> Because he himself suffered when he was tempted, he is able to help those who are being tempted. Let us then approach God's throne of grace with confidence, so that we may receive mercy and find grace to help us in our time of need.
>
> — HEBREWS 2:18, 4:16 (NIV)

6
WHO IS THIS MAN?

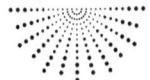

Our television screens nightly show our world's fascination with evil, and many people are looking for spooky experiences that take them beyond the everyday, physical world. However, the Bible declares that evil is neither fun nor fantasy.

READ LUKE 4:31B-37 (WEB)

³³ He was teaching them on the Sabbath ³³ and they were astonished at his teaching, for his word possessed authority. ³³ In the synagogue there was a man who had the spirit of an unclean demon, and he cried out with a loud voice, ³⁴ saying, "Ah! what have you to do with us, Jesus of Nazareth? Have you come to destroy us? I know who you are: the Holy One of God!"

³⁵ Jesus rebuked him, saying, "Be silent, and come out of him!" When the demon had thrown him down in the middle of them, he came out of him, having done him no harm.

³⁶ Amazement came on all, and they said to one another, "What is this teaching? For with authority and

power he commands the unclean spirits, and they come out!" ³⁷ News about him went out into every place in the surrounding region.

EXPLORE

Fresh from His battle with evil in the desert that we read about yesterday, Jesus begins establishing an astonishing ministry.

He wasn't the only teacher travelling around the Jewish synagogues at that time, but Jesus stands out from the crowd. Jewish teachers quoted teachers of the past, but Jesus doesn't need to quote anyone else. He has the authority of God's Spirit (verse 32). Exorcists of that period used elaborate spells and incantations to try to cast out an evil spirit, but Jesus' command is brief, direct, and instantly effective (verse 35).

The people are asking themselves the question: Who is this man? (verses 32,36) The demon, on the other hand, knows exactly who Jesus is (verse 34). However, it doesn't do the demon any good. Knowledge is not the same thing as relationship. The demon's obedience to Jesus is that of a criminal forced at gunpoint into a police car, not the living obedience of true and loving relationship with God.

Do you want to really know this astonishing man, rather than just know about Him? Jesus will open himself to you if you are willing to ask Him. You can ask Him to use His authority and power in your life – but be prepared for amazing things to happen.

ELSEWHERE IN THE BIBLE

The Jewish prophet Daniel foresaw the power and authority of Jesus.

> In my vision at night I looked, and there before me was one like a son of man, coming with the clouds of heaven. He approached the Ancient of Days and was led into his presence. He was given authority, glory and sovereign power; all nations and peoples of every language worshiped him. His dominion is an everlasting dominion that will not pass away, and his kingdom is one that will never be destroyed.
>
> — DANIEL 7:13–14 (NIV)

7
HOLY

Today's society tends to worship celebrities and sports stars, which can disorder the inbuilt human recognition of the holiness of God. Watch Simon Peter's instinctive response when something out-of-this-world happens.

READ LUKE 5:1–11 (WEB)

¹ One day, while the multitude pressed in on him to hear the word of God, he was standing by the lake of Gennesaret. ² He saw two boats by the lake, but the fishermen had gone out of them, and were washing their nets. ³ He got into one of the boats, which was Simon's, and asked him to put out a little from the land. He sat down and taught the people from the boat. ⁴ When he had finished speaking, he said to Simon, "Put out into the deep, and let down your nets for a catch."

⁵ Simon answered him, "Master, we worked all night, and took nothing; but at your word I will let down the net." ⁶ When they had done this, they caught a great multitude of fish, and their net was breaking.

⁷ They signaled to their partners in the other boat to come and help them. They came, and filled both boats, so that they began to sink.

⁸ But Simon Peter, when he saw it, fell down at Jesus' knees, saying, "Depart from me, for I am a sinful man, Lord." ⁹ For he was amazed, and all who were with him, at the catch of fish they had taken; ¹⁰ and so also were James and John, sons of Zebedee, who were partners with Simon.

Jesus said to Simon, "Don't be afraid. From now on you will be catching people."

¹¹ When they had brought their boats to land, they left everything, and followed him.

EXPLORE

Once again, Jesus is teaching (verses 1,3), and once again, we end up asking: Who is this man?

Today we also meet Simon Peter, who would become a leader in the Christian church. But right now, he is tired (verse 5). The experienced fisherman listens to the carpenter's advice (verse 5b), a sure sign that Peter recognized the authority of Jesus.

Peter was probably no worse than the next bloke. But just as most of us look best in soft lighting, most of us feel spiritually okay when we are with people who are about the same as us. For Peter, being in Jesus' presence shone a halogen searchlight into his soul, so that he became painfully aware of every flaw (verse 8).

However, Jesus doesn't condemn him. He tells him to stop being scared, and what's more, He gives him a new job to do (verse 10). The episode is enough to convince Peter and his colleagues to drop everything and follow Jesus (verse 11). Fishing is still a good occupation

– people need to eat – but their priority becomes collecting people for God's kingdom.

Sometimes our unworthiness comes into sharp contrast with God's holiness, and we grieve. However, when we feel bowed down by our sinfulness, God doesn't put His foot on us and hold us there – He gently lifts us up and gives us a worthwhile role to play. If you are feeling unworthy today, ask God to show you His love and compassion and purpose.

ELSEWHERE IN THE BIBLE

The prophet Isaiah had a similar experience when he saw a vision of God.

> "Woe to me!" I cried. "I am ruined! For I am a man of unclean lips, and I live among a people of unclean lips, and my eyes have seen the King, the Lord Almighty."
>
> Then one of the seraphim flew to me with a live coal in his hand, which he had taken with tongs from the altar. With it he touched my mouth and said, "See, this has touched your lips; your guilt is taken away and your sin atoned for."
>
> Then I heard the voice of the Lord saying, "Whom shall I send? And who will go for us?"
>
> And I said, "Here am I. Send me!"
>
> — ISAIAH 6:5–8 (NIV)

8
JESUS THE FORGIVER

Many people carry around burdens of guilt for something that happened in the past. For some of us it's a tiny little thing that no one else even remembers; for others, it can be serious and even criminal. Whichever, it can strangle our relationships and affect our health.

If you are carrying guilt today, you could mime lifting it off your shoulders and placing it at the feet of Jesus, and wait to see what He will do with it as you read today's Bible passage.

READ LUKE 5:18–26 (WEB)

18 Behold, men brought a paralyzed man on a bed, and they sought to bring him in to lay him before Jesus. **19** Not finding a way to bring him in because of the crowd, they went up to the roof, and let him down on his bed through the tiles into the middle before Jesus. **20** Seeing their faith, he said to him, "Man, your sins are forgiven you."

21 The scribes and the Pharisees began to question,

saying, "Who is this who speaks blasphemies? Who can forgive sins, but God alone?"

²² But Jesus, perceiving their thoughts, answered them, "Why are you questioning in your hearts? ²³ Which is easier to say, 'Your sins are forgiven you;' or to say, 'Arise and walk?' ²⁴ But that you may know that the Son of Man has authority on earth to forgive sins" (he said to the paralyzed man), "I tell you, arise, take up your bed, and go home."

²⁵ Immediately he rose up before them, and took up what he had been lying on, and went home, glorifying God. ²⁶ Amazement seized them all, and they glorified God. They were filled with awe, saying, "We have seen extraordinary things today."

EXPLORE

During this era, a paralyzed person needed the help of others to go anywhere. This man's friends are so determined to get him to Jesus that they take him up onto the flat roof of the house and dig their way through the tiles to lower him into the middle of the crowd (verse 19).

It must have caused quite a stir, but the thing that captures Jesus' attention is the faith of all of them (verse 20) – both the paralyzed man and his friends. There are times when all of us need the support of believing friends to carry us, either because our faith or our bodies are not strong enough.

They've come for healing, but Jesus says, "Your sins are forgiven" (verse 20). It seems almost like a change of subject. Once again, we confront the question: Who is this man? This time it is asked by the "scribes and Pharisees," Jesus' opponents in the religious establishment (verse 21) whose power base was threatened by His teachings.

They rightly recognize that God is the only one who can break the power of our sins, but from there they leap to the assumption that Jesus must be blaspheming. The astonishing healing of the man (verse 25) proves that Jesus does indeed speak with God's authority (verse 24).

Unforgiveness between people blocks relationship, and it's the same between us and God. Doctors can cure many illnesses, but only Jesus can restore loving relationship with God. The physical healing of this man was beautiful, but his spiritual healing is a far greater thing.

Remember that burden of guilt we talked about? Will you allow Jesus to take it away from you? He wants to do so. Ask Him about it.

ELSEWHERE IN THE BIBLE

Every person on this planet needs forgiveness, and God is the only one who can give it.

> For as high as the heavens are above the earth, so great is his love for those who fear him; as far as the east is from the west, so far has he removed our transgressions from us.
>
> — PSALM 103:11–12 (NIV)

9
A GENEROUS SPIRIT

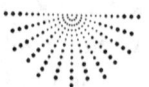

We live in a society whose catchcry is "What about my rights?" Today's reading is going to shake that philosophy to its foundations.

READ LUKE 6:27–38 (WEB)

Jesus said: **27** "But I tell you who hear: love your enemies, do good to those who hate you, **28** bless those who curse you, and pray for those who mistreat you. **29** To one who strikes you on the cheek, offer the other also; and from him who takes away your cloak, don't withhold your tunic also. **30** Give to everyone who asks you, and don't ask anyone who takes away your goods to give them back again.

31 "As you would like people to do to you, do exactly so to them. **32** If you love those who love you, what credit is that to you? For even sinners love those who love them. **33** If you do good to those who do good to you, what credit is that to you? For even sinners do the same. **34** If you lend to those from whom you hope to receive, what credit is that to you? Even sinners lend to sinners, to receive back the same.

³⁵ "But love your enemies, and do good, and lend, expecting nothing back; and your reward will be great, and you will be children of the Most High; for he is kind toward the unthankful and evil.

³⁶ "Therefore be merciful, even as your Father is also merciful.

³⁷ "Don't judge, and you won't be judged. Don't condemn, and you won't be condemned. Forgive, and you will be forgiven.

³⁸ "Give, and it will be given to you: good measure, pressed down, shaken together, and running over, will be poured into your lap. For with the measure you use it will be measured back to you."

EXPLORE

Jesus was a revolutionary. Sayings like "do unto others" and "turn the other cheek" are now cliches, but they originally came from the mouth of Jesus Christ two thousand years ago (verses 31,29). We've lost sight of their shock value. The old Jewish law was "an eye for an eye, and a life for a life." God gave them this law partly to limit evil. For example, two Israelites once slaughtered a whole village after one resident raped their sister. God introduced the rule that the punishment should fit the crime.

But with the advent of Jesus, the Son of God, everything changes. There's no mention of "rights," only responsibilities. Jesus' audience is told to love even enemies (verse 27–28). The time for payback is finished (verse 29).

This is more than morality or behavior. The focus is

not on what the other person deserves, but on who we want to be.

We are to be loving (verses 27,35), merciful and forgiving (verses 28–29,36–37), and generous in every sense (verses 30,35,37–38), so that we can become like our heavenly Father (verses 35–36).

The saying could be reworded, "do unto others as you'd like God to do unto you" or even "be as you'd like God to be." We don't deserve God's love, forgiveness or generosity, and we can be like Him in showing love, forgiveness and generosity towards people who don't deserve it. This is desperately difficult, and we can only ever do it in the power of God's Holy Spirit.

Is there anyone you struggle to forgive? When the hurt is deep, forgiveness can be a wrestling match. You could perhaps start by asking God to help you see that person as He does.

ELSEWHERE IN THE BIBLE

> Therefore, as God's chosen people, holy and dearly loved, clothe yourselves with compassion, kindness, humility, gentleness and patience. Bear with each other and forgive one another if any of you has a grievance against someone. Forgive as the Lord forgave you.
>
> — COLOSSIANS 3:12–13 (NIV)

10
BUILDING STRONG FOUNDATIONS

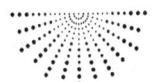

*A*ny engineer will tell you it doesn't matter how beautiful the building is if the foundation won't hold. Building a good foundation for a life is just as crucial. We can add color and style to our existence, but it will fall in a heap if the foundation isn't strong enough.

What is your life founded upon? Think about it as you read this Bible segment.

READ LUKE 6:43–49 (WEB)

Jesus said: **43** "For there is no good tree that produces rotten fruit; nor again a rotten tree that produces good fruit. **44** For each tree is known by its own fruit. For people don't gather figs from thorns, nor do they gather grapes from a bramble bush.

45 "The good man out of the good treasure of his heart produces good, and the evil man out of the evil treasure of his heart brings out that which is evil, for out of the abundance of the heart, his mouth speaks.

46 "Why do you call me, 'Lord, Lord,' and don't do

what I say? ⁴⁷ Everyone who comes to me, and hears my words, and does them, I will show you what he is like. ⁴⁸ He is like a man building a house, who dug and went deep, and laid a foundation on the rock. When a flood arose, the stream broke against that house, and could not shake it, because it was founded on the rock. ⁴⁹ But he who hears, and doesn't do, is like a man who built a house on the ground without a foundation. When the stream broke against it, immediately it fell, and the ruin of that house was great."

EXPLORE

Jesus says life is like gardening. If you want strawberries, don't plant cabbages (verse 44), or you're bound to be disappointed – as will everyone who eats your jam!

If, like me, you ever regret things you've said, Jesus offers sound advice. What we say will be flavored by what we read, watch, and listen to. What are we "planting" in our minds? We need to actively and eagerly seek good input, because what comes out of our mouths is what has gone into our hearts (verse 45).

Jesus says life is like housing construction (verses 48–49). I once saw a house where the land had subsided, causing cracks and leaks. It had probably been hard to tell the land wasn't going to hold firm. Sometimes the things we have built our lives upon can look solid and dependable – a first class job, a loving family. But then recession comes or someone dies or rejects us, and it falls apart.

Our lives need to be built to hurrican/earthquake standard, with the deepest and strongest foundation possible – relationship with God through Jesus.

The key is in verse 47. If we listen to Jesus' words to

us through the Bible, absorb them into our hearts, and live them out in our words and actions, we will be strong and fruitful, even in the face of the worst hardship or the strongest opposition.

As you go through this day, think about what you are putting your trust in, and what is going into your heart. If you are willing, ask God to help you to anchor your life in Him.

ELSEWHERE IN THE BIBLE

> Blessed is the one who trusts in the LORD, whose confidence is in him. They will be like a tree planted by the water that sends out its roots by the stream. It does not fear when heat comes; its leaves are always green. It has no worries in a year of drought and never fails to bear fruit.
>
> —JEREMIAH 17:7–8 (NIV)

11

LORD OF CREATION

I grew up in a sailing family, and as we were prone to staying on the island "just a little longer" we were regularly caught in the vicious late afternoon storms that whipped Moreton Bay into a frenzy. As a poor swimmer and embarrassingly unheroic, I would scurry below decks, wrap myself in a huge yellow lifejacket, and pray. My brother, meanwhile, would get a glint in his eye and spring into action.

Today we're going to read about sailors who find themselves engulfed by a cataclysmic storm, but they are even more terrified by what stops the storm. Ask God to help you understand how their story might be relevant to your life.

READ LUKE 8:22–25 (WEB)

22 One day, he got into a boat, himself and his disciples, and he said to them, "Let's go over to the other side of the lake." So they launched out. **23** As they sailed, he fell asleep. A wind storm came down on the lake, and they were filling with water and were in danger.

24 They went and woke him, saying, "Master, master, we are dying!" He awoke, and rebuked the wind and the raging waters, and they ceased, and it was calm. **25** He said to them, "Where is your faith?" They were afraid and they marveled, saying to one another, "Who is this then, that he commands even the winds and the water, and they obey him?"

EXPLORE

Once again, Luke gets us asking his theme question: Who *is* this man?

There were other teachers around whose passionate speeches could draw large crowds. There were magicians who could perform impressive tricks, including apparent healings. But today's incident sets Jesus well apart from any of His contemporaries.

The lake of Galilee is renowned for its sudden storms. Winds sweep down from the surrounding mountains and in a moment a sunny day becomes a maelstrom. Several of Jesus' disciples were professional fishermen, so this storm must have been something special to throw these old salts into a panic.

Their words to Jesus (verse 24) could mean several things. "How can you sleep through this?" Or: "Do something!" Or even: "Get ready to swim for it!"

Whatever the disciples were asking for, they clearly did not expect what they got: instant calm. Their terror transfers from the storm to Jesus, as they realize just who is in the boat with them.

Only God can stop a storm.

Jesus rebukes not just the storm (verse 24) – but the disciples as well (verse 25). His question might mean: "Where has your faith gone?" Or it could mean: "In what do you put your faith?" In either case, it is a challenge to stop trusting in their own ability as expert sailors and trust the one who made the sea.

God is bigger than anything that could happen to you. If you are in the midst of a storm right now, ask Him to get in the boat with you. To hold you tight, to give you His peace, and to guide you safely to shore.

ELSEWHERE IN THE BIBLE

The ancient Jewish poets recognized that only God could control the weather.

> Who is like you, LORD God Almighty? You, LORD, are mighty, and your faithfulness surrounds you. You rule over the surging sea; when its waves mount up, you still them.
>
> — PSALM 89:8–9 (NIV)

12

BEING SEEN AT LAST

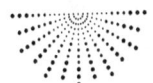

Chronic illness, including mental health issues, can be physically, financially and emotionally draining. The same was true in the first century AD. What does Jesus think about it?

READ LUKE 8:43–48 (WEB)

⁴³ A woman who had a flow of blood for twelve years, who had spent all her living on physicians and could not be healed by any ⁴⁴ came up behind him, and touched the fringe of his cloak. Immediately her flow of blood stopped. ⁴⁵ Jesus said, "Who touched me?"

When all denied it, Peter said, "Master, the crowds press and jostle you.'"

⁴⁶ But Jesus said, "Someone did touch me, for I perceive that power has gone out of me." ⁴⁷ When the woman saw that she was not hidden, she came trembling, and falling down before him declared in the presence of all the people the reason why she had touched him, and how she was healed immediately. ⁴⁸ He said to

her, "Daughter, your faith has made you well. Go in peace."

EXPLORE

Jesus is being crushed by the crowds (verse 42), and this woman has been crushed by her medical condition for twelve long years (verse 43). Anemia must have been draining her energy as much as her finances, as she has endured the hope/despair cycle so familiar to those of us seeking effective treatment for chronic illness.

At this time, a person who was bleeding was excluded from general society and religious fellowship. Today, isolation is still a common wound for the chronically ill, when they have not the strength for social events or the workforce, and are even accused of being lazy or negative.

It's unlikely that this woman would have felt free to come up to Jesus during the public healings. She may have been embarrassed to speak about a "women's problem," and it may even have been against the rules for her to be in that crowd.

So, in her desperation, she tries for a secret healing (verse 44), not bothering the teacher.

But there's not going to be a secret healing. Jesus insists that she declare herself (verses 45–46). In other instances, Jesus knew the thoughts in people's hearts, so perhaps He knew who had touched Him and why. Perhaps His insistence is not based on His need to know, but her need to be seen at last, and for the crowd to see how he treats her.

She could still have run away, but instead she tells the full story of what Jesus has done for her (verse 47).

With her public declaration comes public vindication. Jesus does not scold but speaks tenderly to her. He has given her physical healing, social healing and, most importantly, spiritual healing (verse 48).

I have witnessed miraculous physical healings in Jesus' name in my lifetime, but also many more cases where it didn't happen. Divine physical healing is not some heavenly slot-machine but a mystery. Please resist anyone who makes disparaging declarations about why some people are healed and some are not.

Relationship with God through Jesus, however, is the greatest miracle, and available to all, simply for the asking.

If you have good health, ask God to help you understand how invisibility and exclusion might be affecting someone you know and what you could do about it. If you live with chronic illness, you are seen by Jesus, and He cares deeply about every aspect of your situation. You are not "bothering Him" when you reach out to Him with all your concerns.

ELSEWHERE IN THE BIBLE

> The LORD is close to the brokenhearted and saves those who are crushed in spirit.
>
> — PSALM 34:18 (NIV)

13
WHO AM I?

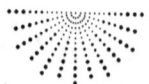

I talk to many people who have a vague and woolly idea that Jesus was a "good man" (although their opinion is not usually based on research). His love for outsiders and His fearless opposition to corruption sometimes make Him a poster boy for various action groups, who regard His death as a miscarriage of justice and use it to highlight modern-day injustices. (Spoiler alert: His death is much more than that.)

Thanks to the Bible we have a record of what Jesus said and did, so today we're going to investigate who Jesus believed He was and what His death was about. You might like to pause and ask God for insight before you read.

READ LUKE 9:18–22 (WEB)

[18] As he was praying alone, the disciples were with him, and he asked them, "Who do the crowds say that I am?"

[19] They answered, "'John the Baptist,' but others say,

'Elijah,' and others, that one of the prophets of old has risen again."

20 He said to them, "But who do you say that I am?"

Peter answered, "The Christ of God."

21 But he warned them, and commanded them to tell this to no one, **22** saying, "The Son of Man must suffer many things, and be rejected by the elders, chief priests, and scribes, and be killed, and on the third day be raised up."

EXPLORE

This time Jesus Himself is asking the "Who is this man?" question (verse 18).

Just like us, Jesus' contemporaries had many different ideas about His identity (verse 19). The story turns on Peter's revelation in verse 20: He is the Christ of God. Peter's knowledge is not the product of rumors. It stems from a personal relationship with the man in question, and insight given to Peter by God.

"Christ" is a Greek word meaning someone anointed by God with His Spirit for a special task. Jesus is not just *an* anointed one. He is *the* anointed one (verse 20).

Although the disciples are right about this, Jesus warns them to keep it to themselves for now (verse 21). He generally prefers to call himself the Son of Man (verse 22). The word "Christ" had become politically loaded because the Jews wanted the Christ to free them from the oppression of the Roman Empire through a military victory.

Jesus explains to His inner circle that something quite different and in fact much bigger is required of the Christ (verse 22). It would have been puzzling and distressing news, and they will never really understand it until after Jesus' death and resurrection.

Put simply, the world's rejection of God earned it the death penalty. Because God loved us so much that he'd rather die than live without us, Jesus came to take the death penalty on our behalf. His resurrection is the evidence that the plan worked.

It can take time to fully grasp these mysterious truths. Don't be afraid to talk to God about it.

ELSEWHERE IN THE BIBLE

> But he was pierced for our transgressions, he was crushed for our iniquities; the punishment that brought us peace was on him, and by his wounds we are healed. We all, like sheep, have gone astray, each of us has turned to our own way; and the Lord has laid on him the iniquity of us all.
>
> — ISAIAH 53:5–6 (NIV)

14
LIFE GOALS THAT TRULY SATISFY

We live in an "eat dessert first," "do whatever makes you happy" kind of world, but also see people give up many things to, say, climb Mt Everest or qualify for the Olympics. Today's message is more Mt Everest Christianity than Cake Christianity, and it can be hard to hear. May I invite you to read with an open mind and heart, and ask God to help you understand what it might mean for you?

READ LUKE 9:23-26 (WEB)

23 He said to all, "If anyone desires to come after me, let him deny himself, take up his cross daily, and follow me. 24 For whoever desires to save his life will lose it, but whoever loses his life for my sake, will save it. 25 For what does it profit a man if he gains the whole world, and loses or forfeits his own self? 26 For whoever is ashamed of me and of my words, of him will the Son of Man be ashamed, when he comes in his glory, and the glory of the Father, and of the holy angels."

EXPLORE

Remember that the disciples received this message during a tough time. They've just heard that the role of the Messiah is a brutal death, not political victory. Now they learn that their role is not to act as His powerful lieutenants in a military coup, but to follow their leader down the path of suffering and sacrifice (verse 23).

Verse 24 contains hints of martyrdom, and it certainly turned out that way for that small group gathered around Jesus. Many early Christian leaders died for their faith.

This message is as serious as it gets.

In the western world at the time of writing, persecution is rarely fatal, but the principles apply in other ways. I knew a brilliant surgeon who could have enjoyed luxurious prestige but chose instead to take his (willing) young family to a dirty and dangerous developing country where he could use his medical skills to show God's love. To outsiders, it appeared that he had lost his life for the sake of Jesus – but he told a very different story of a life truly worth living.

Jesus doesn't want just the available bits of us, or even the best bits. He wants everything – all the mess. He wants to be more important to us than anything else in life, even than oxygen. When that happens, we find an astonishing life full of meaning.

It is an adventure, but it is also sometimes painful. We fail, we forget, we try to clutch at the cake-life we thought we wanted, but He is patient and forgiving. Turning us into the people we are becoming is a life's work.

Is there anything in your life you don't want to give up for the sake of Jesus? You might like to discuss it with

God right now. He already knows what it is, so don't be afraid to tell Him how you really feel. See what happens.

ELSEWHERE IN THE BIBLE

Paul, one of the early Christian leaders, was in prison for his faith when he wrote:

> I consider that our present sufferings are not worth comparing with the glory that will be revealed in us.
>
> — ROMANS 8:18 (NIV)

15
BEING BUSY VERSUS JUST BEING

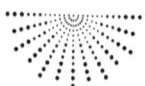

*L*ife is getting busier and busier, and every day seems full of distractions. Take a few deep breaths and exhale slowly as you try to focus your mind on what you are about to read. Read it through several times if it helps you to concentrate.

READ LUKE 10:38–42 (WEB)

38 As they went on their way, he entered into a village, and a woman named Martha welcomed him into her house. **39** She had a sister called Mary, who sat at Jesus' feet, and heard his word. **40** But Martha was distracted with much serving, and she went up to him, and said, "Lord, don't you care that my sister has left me to serve alone? Ask her therefore to help me."

41 Jesus answered her, "Martha, Martha, you are anxious and troubled about many things, **42** but one thing is needed. Mary has chosen the good portion, which will not be taken away from her."

EXPLORE

I confess I feel a bit sorry for Martha. The whole Jesus Tour has arrived on her doorstep (verse 38), all needing to be fed and rested, and there's a lot to do to make that happen. She can't believe that Mary would leave the work to her (verse 40).

There is possibly an element of challenging gender expectations here – in those days, women were supposed to do the housework, and men were supposed to learn theology. But the main message of Jesus' reply (verses 41–42) seems to be that Martha's feverish activity has blinded her to what really matters (verse 40).

What Jesus would most like to be presented with is not a gourmet meal, but an open and teachable heart. The most important behavior for a disciple of Jesus is not admirable purposeful activity, but being in His presence, listening.

Our actions do matter, as a sign of our response to Jesus' free gift of loving relationship with God. But in the end, Christianity is not about what we do but who we are. If you have chosen to follow Jesus, you are a beloved child of the Lord of the universe, and that is worth sitting and thinking about.

If you have become a Christian, you will instinctively want to do things that please God, and that's good, but make sure that you also take time out just to "be." Wallow in His presence and soak up His love for you. Some people find it meaningful to express this through conversation with God, and others prefer arts such as poetry, painting or song.

ELSEWHERE IN THE BIBLE

King David, ancestor of Jesus, knew the joy of God's presence.

> One thing I ask from the Lord, this only do I seek: that I may dwell in the house of the Lord all the days of my life, to gaze on the beauty of the Lord and to seek him in his temple.
>
> — PSALM 27:4 (NIV)

16
HOW TO PRAY

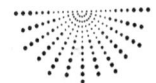

We often don't know how to pray, but the wonderful thing is, God is happy to teach and inspire us.

READ LUKE 11:1–13 (WEB)

When he finished praying in a certain place, one of his disciples said to him, "Lord, teach us to pray, just as John also taught his disciples."

² He said to them, "When you pray, say,

'Our Father in heaven,

may your name be kept holy.

May your Kingdom come.

May your will be done on earth, as it is in heaven.

³ Give us day by day our daily bread.

⁴ Forgive us our sins, for we ourselves also forgive everyone who is indebted to us.

Bring us not into temptation.'"

⁵ He said to them, "Which of you, if you go to a friend at midnight, and tell him, 'Friend, lend me three loaves of bread, ⁶ for a friend of mine has come to me

from a journey, and I have nothing to set before him,' ⁷ will answer from inside and say, 'Don't bother me. The door is now shut, and my children and I are in bed. I can't get up and give it to you'? ⁸ I tell you, although he will not rise and give it to him because he is his friend, yet because of his persistence, he will get up and give him as much as he needs.

⁹ "I tell you, keep asking, and it will be given you. Keep seeking, and you will find. Keep knocking, and it will be opened to you. ¹⁰ For everyone who asks receives. The one who seeks finds. To the one who knocks it will be opened.

¹¹ "Which of you fathers, if your son asks for a fish, will give him a snake instead? ¹² Or if he asks for an egg, will give him a scorpion? ¹³ If you then, though you are evil, know how to give good gifts to your children, how much more will your heavenly Father give the Holy Spirit to those who ask him?"

EXPLORE

Some people make prayer seem like an incantation or a ritual, but Jesus' instructions on the subject were straightforward. It is a conversation based on intimate relationship, and Jesus gave a good example by His own constant prayerfulness (eg verse 1).

He told His disciples what to pray, how to pray, and what to expect. Verses 2–4 provide the basic structure of the Lord's Prayer, which has become well-known in many parts of the world. It shows us the type of things He wants us to ask for – we don't necessarily have to use these exact words. We are to ask for the world to respond appropriately to God (verse 2), for the provision of our daily needs (verse 3), that we might be forgiven and forgiving, and for help in avoiding temptation (verse 4).

Verses 5–10 reveal the spirit in which we should pray. Jesus is not telling us that God is reluctant to get out of His warm bed to hear our requests. The focus of this little tale is *our* behavior, not God's. We are to be persistent and bold in asking God for what we need (verses 8–10), persevering until we reach a resolution.

Verses 9–13 tell us what to expect, based on the character of God, not our worthiness. If the average human parent doesn't give a child something poisonous when they're hungry, how much more can we expect of an all-good, all-loving Father-God?

God is a generous Father who delights in giving good things to His children. God's idea of good won't always coincide with ours, however. I may have happily eaten chocolate all day as a child, but thankfully my mother gave me meat and bread and vegetables. In the same way, God will give us what is best for us; notice His good and generous gift of the Holy Spirit (verse 13).

We can confidently ask God for the things He has told us to ask for.

ELSEWHERE IN THE BIBLE

> Rejoice always, pray continually, give thanks in all circumstances; for this is God's will for you in Christ Jesus.
>
> —1 THESSALONIANS 5:16–18 (NIV)

17
DIFFERENT KINDS OF FEAR

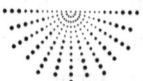

Our society often portrays God as a benevolent white-bearded old man who sits on a cloud waiting to bestow indulgent smiles on His naughty but lovable children.

Their "god" is harmless and ineffectual. He is nothing like the God of the Bible. Ask God to help you understand His holiness today.

READ LUKE 12:1–7 (WEB)

¹ Meanwhile, when a multitude of many thousands had gathered together, so much so that they trampled on each other, he began to speak first to his disciples, saying, "Beware of the yeast of the Pharisees, which is hypocrisy. ² But there is nothing concealed that will not be revealed, nor hidden that will not be made known. ³ Therefore whatever you have said in the darkness will be heard in the light. What you have whispered in the ear in the inner rooms will be proclaimed on the housetops.

⁴ "I tell you, my friends, don't be afraid of those who

kill the body, and after that have no more that they can do. ⁵ But I will warn you whom you should fear. Fear him who after your body has been killed, has power to cast into Gehenna [hell]. Yes, I tell you, fear him.

⁶ "Aren't five sparrows sold for two assaria coins? Yet not one of them is forgotten by God. ⁷ But the very hairs of your head are all numbered. Therefore don't be afraid. You are of more value than many sparrows."

EXPLORE

I've been afraid of lots of things in my life. Spiders. Oversleeping on exam day. Mosquito-borne diseases. Muggers in dark alleys. My fears have varying levels of intensity and accuracy. However, today's lesson from Jesus is that even the things that are worth being afraid of are nothing, compared to God.

The greatest human fear is death (verse 4), but Jesus points out that even a murderer's power is limited. They can take the life from your body, but they can't have any impact on your eternity. Only God will decide your eternal fate, and His power is absolute (verse 5). He is the only one worth fearing.

He hates hypocrisy, which seeps into every part of life, like yeast through a lump of dough (verse 1). He singles out religious leaders (in verse 1, "the Pharisees") who love rules more than people and put on a show that doesn't match their secret thoughts and behaviors. To say one thing and do another might fool people for a time, but God is not fooled, and the day is coming when every two-faced person will be exposed for all the world to see (verses 2–3).

But the astonishingly good news is that this fearsome God is on our side (verses 6–7). He knows everything about you, even the number of hairs on your head, and still He treasures you.

Our God is no old dodderer sitting on a cloud. He is very scary indeed. But He also has a fierce and protective love for you. It is worth spending a little time in quiet reverence, soaking up this amazing truth.

ELSEWHERE IN THE BIBLE

The prophet Isaiah understood that God is not "safe," but He is our only safe haven.

> This is what the LORD says to me with his strong hand upon me, warning me not to follow the way of this people: "Do not call conspiracy everything this people calls a conspiracy; do not fear what they fear, and do not dread it. The LORD Almighty is the one you are to regard as holy, he is the one you are to fear, he is the one you are to dread. He will be a holy place."
>
> — ISAIAH 8:11–14 (NIV)

18

TRUE COMFORT IN ANXIETY

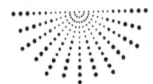

Are you worried about anything today? Ask God to help you take a break to focus fully on Him right now.

READ LUKE 12:15, 23–26, 29–34 (WEB)

15 He said to them, "Beware! Keep yourselves from covetousness, for a man's life doesn't consist of the abundance of the things he possesses.

23 "Life is more than food, and the body is more than clothing. 24 Consider the ravens: they don't sow, they don't reap, they have no warehouse or barn, and God feeds them. How much more valuable are you than birds!

25 "Which of you by being anxious can add a cubit to his height? 26 If then you aren't able to do even the least things, why are you anxious about the rest?

29 "Don't set your heart on what you will eat or what you will drink; neither be anxious. 30 For the nations of the world seek after all of these things, but your Father knows that you need these things.

[31] "But seek God's Kingdom, and all these things will be added to you. [32] Don't be afraid, little flock, for it is your Father's good pleasure to give you the Kingdom. [33] Sell your possessions and give gifts to the needy. Make for yourselves purses which don't grow old, a treasure in the heavens that doesn't fail, where no thief approaches, neither moth destroys. [34] For where your treasure is, there will your heart be also."

EXPLORE

First-century society was just as focused on wealth and possessions as ours is today (verse 30). Jesus declares what many a millionaire has realized on their deathbed: We are not defined by what we own (verse 15), and money can't buy the breath of life (verse 25).

Compared to grasping after more and greater possessions, worrying about not being able to pay the electricity bill might seem to be in a totally different category, but Jesus groups them together. Both pursuing wealth and fearing poverty involve setting our sights on something other than Jesus.

The message is that whether we own much or little in the material sense, Christians are all fabulously wealthy in the spiritual sense. We own something infinitely precious that can never depreciate or be taken away from us (verse 33). We are beloved children of God, heirs of the King of the universe (verse 32). We are to be responsible citizens of this world, but our focus is on citizenship of another world.

Jesus' advice to hold lightly to our possessions can also apply to other areas of life. We can frantically pursue good health, family togetherness, career achievements. And conversely, we can worry incessantly about the lack of such things. Either approach is to make a god of something other than Jesus.

Most of us struggle at times against materialism, whether we are rich or poor. You might find it helpful to mime handing over your possessions and your money worries to God.

ELSEWHERE IN THE BIBLE

King David knew both wealth and poverty, but God remained his deepest longing.

> As the deer pants for streams of water, so my soul pants for you, my God. My soul thirsts for God, for the living God. When can I go and meet with God?
>
> — PSALM 42:1–2 (NIV)

19

OPPOSITION IS EXPECTED

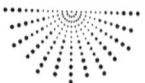

In a church in a former communist country, I sat on a hard wooden bench next to people who had spent years in mental asylums for their faith, betrayed by their own family members. They had clung to Jesus through every attempt to make them let go – and he had hung on just as firmly to them. These people truly knew the value of relationship with Jesus, and I was deeply challenged by their clarity and tenacity.

If anyone or anything is trying to make you let go of Jesus, or persuade you not to grab hold of Him in the first place, ask God to strengthen you through His message to you today.

READ LUKE 12:49–53 (WEB)

Jesus said: **49** "I came to throw fire on the earth. I wish it were already kindled. **50** But I have a baptism to undergo, and how distressed I am until it is accomplished! **51** Do you think that I have come to bring peace in the earth? I tell you, no, but rather division. **52** For from now on, there will be five in one house divided, three against two, and two against three. **⁵³** They will be divided, father against son, and son against father; mother against daughter, and daughter against mother; mother-in-law against her daughter-in-law, and daughter-in-law against mother-in-law."

EXPLORE

If you're facing opposition for your decision to follow Jesus, please understand that this doesn't mean there's something wrong with you. All Christians face opposition at some time in our lives. Depending on the culture, persecution can include anything from teasing and contempt to loss of job opportunities and marriage prospects, or even death.

Jesus came to bring peace between God and humankind, but this very action created hostility between people (verse 51). This is because those who want to pursue peace with God are travelling in a completely opposite direction to those who don't, and friction results.

Jesus suffered the ultimate persecution. The baptism of fire that He is anticipating (verses 49–50) is His death on the cross. This is how Jesus would deal with every single action of rebellion against God since the beginning of the world.

A woman longs for the birth of her baby, even though labor is painful and unpleasant, because there will be a cherished child at the end of it. In an even more powerful way, Jesus longs for His sacrificial death to come, even though it will be a horrifying experience, because the end result will be the salvation of the world.

I don't know what opposition you might be facing, but Jesus does. Ask Him for strength. If you are holding back from committing yourself to Jesus because you're afraid of how others might react, ask God for courage and wisdom.

ELSEWHERE IN THE BIBLE

This writer was in constant danger because of his faith.

> What, then, shall we say in response to these things? If God is for us, who can be against us? He who did not spare his own Son, but gave him up for us all—how will he not also, along with him, graciously give us all things? For I am convinced that neither death nor life, neither angels nor demons, neither the present nor the future, nor any powers, neither height nor depth, nor anything else in all creation, will be able to separate us from the love of God that is in Christ Jesus our Lord.
>
> — ROMANS 8:31–32, 38–39 (NIV)

20

ONE WAY

Christianity, or God's kingdom or relationship with God, is like a warm, bright house, spilling light out into a cold, dark place. Some people will circle the house for years, looking in the windows and yearning for the love and relationships that are inside. There is only one door, and it stands open, and Jesus is at the door holding out His arms in welcome.

But sometimes people are afraid He'll ask them to leave some of their baggage at the door, so they stay out in the cold. Jesus said that the day will come when the door is shut. If you're still circling, please don't be outside then.

READ LUKE 13:23-30 (WEB)

23 Someone asked him, "Lord, are they few who will be saved?"

He said to them, 24 "Strive to enter in by the narrow door, for many, I tell you, will seek to enter in and will not be able. 25 When once the master of the house has risen up, and has shut the door, and you begin to stand outside and to knock at the door, saying, 'Lord, Lord, open to us!' then he will answer you, 'I don't know where you come from.' ²⁶ Then you will begin to say, 'We ate and drank in your presence, and you taught in our streets.' ²⁷ He will say, 'I tell you, I don't know where you come from. Depart from me, all you workers of evil.' ²⁸ There will be weeping and gnashing of teeth when you see Abraham, Isaac, Jacob, and all the prophets in the kingdom of God, but yourselves thrown outside. ²⁹ People will come from the east, west, north, and south, and will sit down at the table in God's Kingdom. ³⁰ Behold, there are some who are last who will be first, and there are some who are first who will be last."

EXPLORE

Someone asks Jesus whether only the best people are going to be saved (verse 23). Jesus dismisses this spiritual snobbery with a straightforward answer containing three unpalatable truths.

First, He says there is only one way into God's kingdom, one narrow door, and we don't get to choose our own entry point. Jesus is both the narrow door (verse 24) and the owner of the house (the owner is the one who "taught in our streets" – verse 26).

Second, He says that some people who think they'll be "in" have a surprise coming (verse 30). Being a good Jew (or a good churchgoer, or a good person) is no entry pass. Brushing past Jesus on the way through life doesn't qualify. According to Jesus, only those who actually *know* Jesus will be admitted to heaven (verse 25).

Third, He says that being outside of heaven is not the fun get-together that some people joke about, but a place of torment and regret (verse 28).

I find these truths troubling, because I want everybody to be in relationship with God and go to heaven. But the thing is, God put that desire in my heart because it's what He wants too. He wants everybody to come in and have a loving relationship with Him, but He won't force them. And if God hadn't sent Jesus, there would have been no way in.

If you've been brushing past Jesus for years, get to know Him, starting now. If you are finding it hard to accept Jesus' assertion that He is the only way to God, talk to Him honestly about it.

ELSEWHERE IN THE BIBLE

Jesus said:

> "Do not let your hearts be troubled. You believe in God; believe also in me. My Father's house has many rooms; if that were not so, would I have told you that I am going there to prepare a place for you? And if I go and prepare a place for you, I will come back and take you to be with me that you also may be where I am. I am the way and the truth and the life. No one comes to the Father except through me."
>
> — JOHN 14:1–3, 6 (NIV)

21

COUNTING THE COST

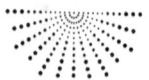

Have you ever done anything that was truly worthwhile? What did it cost you? Think about not just finances, but time, relationships, other opportunities that you sidelined in order to pursue the goal. How much would you be willing to give up in order to pursue life with Jesus?

READ LUKE 14:26–33 (WEB)

Jesus said: **26** "If anyone comes to me, and doesn't hate his own father, mother, wife, children, brothers, and sisters, yes, and his own life also, he can't be my disciple. **27** Whoever doesn't bear his own cross, and come after me, can't be my disciple.

28 "For which of you, desiring to build a tower, doesn't first sit down and count the cost, to see if he has enough to complete it? **29** Otherwise, when he has laid a foundation, and is not able to finish, everyone who sees begins to mock him, **30** saying, 'This man began to build, and wasn't able to finish.'

31 "Or what king, as he goes to encounter another

king in war, will not sit down first and consider whether he is able with ten thousand to meet him who comes against him with twenty thousand? **32** If not, while the other is yet a great way off, he sends a delegation, and asks for terms of peace.

33 "So therefore any one of you who doesn't renounce all that he has cannot be my disciple."

EXPLORE

These words from Jesus are shocking, and He means them to be. He wants to jolt us into realizing that He must be the most important thing in our lives. Christian faith cannot work any other way. It is not a hobby or special interest but a life force. We must loosen our grip on everything else that we thought was important and give Jesus central place (verse 33), so that everything else falls into its correct position. It's hard!

Jesus is not saying that we should behave cruelly towards our family, any more than that we should construct a large wooden cross and drag it around with us every day (verse 27). The Bible must always be read in context, and in other places Jesus tells us that we are responsible to care for our family members in a godly way. As He was dying, He even made arrangements for one of His disciples to care for Jesus' own mother.

Rather, He is using a figure of speech to make His point. Our love for Jesus should be so strong that our love for our family and even our own lives looks like hatred by comparison (verse 26).

Sometimes this love will override other things that we may have liked to do. Jesus wants to be more important to us than even the most precious and beautiful things of this life.

If you are willing, symbolically hand over to Jesus all the things you treasure most, and wait to see what He will return to you.

ELSEWHERE IN THE BIBLE

Paul, the early Christian leader, was a highly respected member of the community... until he chose Jesus and became an outlaw.

> But whatever were gains to me I now consider loss for the sake of Christ. What is more, I consider everything a loss because of the surpassing worth of knowing Christ Jesus my Lord, for whose sake I have lost all things. I consider them garbage, that I may gain Christ.
>
> — PHILIPPIANS 3:7–8 (NIV)

22
YOU ARE PRECIOUS!

The story goes that a man dropped his car keys at night and was hunting for them under a streetlight. A passerby stopped to help, and asked, "Where exactly did you drop them?"

"Over there," the man said, pointing into the darkness.

"Then why are we looking over here?" asked his puzzled helper.

"Because there's more light over here," the man replied.

My natural inclination is to stay in my comfort zone, but the challenge from Jesus is to go to the darkest places to search for lost people.

READ LUKE 15:1–10 (WEB)

¹ Now all the tax collectors and sinners were coming close to him to hear him. ² The Pharisees and the scribes murmured, saying, "This man welcomes sinners, and eats with them."

³ He told them this parable. ⁴ "Which of you, if you

had one hundred sheep, and lost one of them, wouldn't leave the ninety-nine in the open country, and go after the one that was lost, until he finds it? ⁵ When he has found it, he carries it on his shoulders, rejoicing. ⁶ When he comes home, he calls together his friends and his neighbors, saying to them, 'Rejoice with me, for I have found my sheep which was lost!'

⁷ "I tell you that in the same way there will be more joy in heaven over one sinner who repents, than over ninety-nine righteous people who need no repentance.

⁸ "Or what woman, if she had ten silver coins, if she lost one coin, wouldn't light a lamp, sweep the house, and seek diligently until she found it? ⁹ When she has found it, she calls together her friends and neighbors, saying, 'Rejoice with me, for I have found the coin I had lost.'

¹⁰ "In the same way, I tell you, there is joy in the presence of the angels of God over one sinner repenting."

EXPLORE

Jesus spent a lot of time in the company of undesirable people. They were drawn to Him, like iron filings to a magnet (verse 1), and He did not send them away.

The religious leaders were far from happy about this (verse 2). To their way of thinking, a religious teacher and community leader should not encourage friendships with people whose morals were questionable. Jesus was setting a bad example. Imagine a modern-day archbishop photographed dining out with criminals.

However, Jesus answers their criticism, as He so often does, with stories. In these stories, the people who do not think they need to repent (verse 7, compare the sheep of verse 4) are being aligned with the Pharisees. They think they are righteous. (They're not.)

Jesus seeks people who know they're lost and want to be found. He is not by his choice of companions endorsing sinful behavior but revealing the yearning heart of God, who is ecstatic when one person turns back to Him.

There are many examples in the Bible where people with doubtful pasts turned to Jesus and started over again. There are similar examples in life today. You may be one of them. Whatever your past, you are exquisitely precious to God.

If you have turned to God, there has been a party in heaven in celebration over you (verse 10). Allow yourself to feel God's joy today. If you are still thinking about it, know that God is reaching out to you because you are precious.

ELSEWHERE IN THE BIBLE

God told the prophet Isaiah how much He yearned for people who were far from worthy.

> "I revealed myself to those who did not ask for me; I was found by those who did not seek me. To a nation that did not call on my name, I said, 'Here am I, here am I.' All day long I have held out my hands to an obstinate people, who walk in ways not good, pursuing their own imaginations."
>
> — ISAIAH 65:1–2 (NIV)

23
CALLED TO BE FORGIVEN AND FORGIVING

I read an interview with a Christian woman who found healing in forgiving the man who murdered her husband in a random act of violence – such a challenging story. I once experienced a significant betrayal by someone in authority who did not repent; I worked hard to forgive them, but for years the same old emotions would erupt in the middle of a sleepless night, and I would ask God to forgive my unforgiveness and help me forgive again.

Forgiveness is not always straightforward, is it? If there is a deep hurt weighing on you today, ask God to comfort you and show you what to do.

READ LUKE 17:1–6 (WEB)

¹ He said to the disciples, "It is impossible that no temptations to sin should come, but woe to him through whom they come! ² It would be better for him if a millstone were hung around his neck, and he were thrown into the sea, rather than that he should cause one of these little ones to stumble.

³ "Watch yourselves. If your brother sins against you, rebuke him. If he repents, forgive him. ⁴ If he sins against you seven times in a day, and seven times returns, saying, 'I repent,' you must forgive him."

⁵ The apostles said to the Lord, "Increase our faith."

⁶ The Lord said, "If you had faith like a grain of mustard seed, you would tell this mulberry tree, 'Be uprooted, and planted in the sea,' and it would obey you."

EXPLORE

I tremble to see how seriously Jesus viewed the sin of leading someone astray (verses 1–2). Maybe I haven't led anyone into a life of crime, but have I, even accidentally, influenced anyone to ignore the teachings of Jesus? Worldwide, churches are fracturing, fulfilling this prediction: "For the time will come when people will not put up with sound doctrine. Instead, to suit their own desires, they will gather around them a great number of teachers to say what their itching ears want to hear." (2 Timothy 4:3 NIV)

Jesus speaks quite bluntly about our responsibilities within the Christian family – we must help one another stay on track (verses 1,3) and have nothing to do with bitterness (verses 3–4).

Christians, even the really nice ones, do hurt each other, sometimes deeply. Resentment is a natural human reaction, but any psychologist will tell you how toxic it can be to our mental health. God, who designed us, knows that letting go will do us good, but also has a deeper spiritual concern: unforgiveness draws our focus and energy away from God's priorities.

When we choose to forgive, we're not saying that the

hurtful action didn't matter. We're refusing to retaliate. We're deciding not to deliberately hang on to our pain but to focus our finite reserves of energy elsewhere.

Just like us, the disciples seem to realize how difficult this will be and ask Jesus to increase their faith (verse 5). Jesus has a double-edged answer. You don't need a huge faith, just do it; but you'll also be surprised how much a small faith can achieve (verse 6).

Do you need to forgive, or ask someone for forgiveness? See if you can find the courage to confront it. If it is very hard, tell God, and ask Him to help you.

ELSEWHERE IN THE BIBLE

Jesus does not ask more of us than of Himself.

> When they came to the place called the Skull, they crucified him there, along with the criminals—one on his right, the other on his left. Jesus said, "Father, forgive them, for they do not know what they are doing." And they divided up his clothes by casting lots.
>
> — LUKE 23:33–34 (NIV)

24
DON'T HOLD BACK

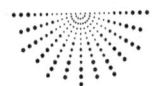

When I was a young journalist, I went to a press conference for Torville and Dean, the Olympic ice dancers. I desperately wanted to ask for an autograph, but I was afraid the experienced and cynical journalists around me would sneer. So I didn't do it. I've often regretted that – and it was only an autograph!

Don't let peer pressure stop you grabbing hold of the things that will really matter for the rest of your life and all eternity.

READ LUKE 18:35–43 (WEB)

35 As he came near Jericho, a certain blind man was sitting by the road, begging. 36 Hearing a crowd going by, he asked what this meant. 37 They told him, "Jesus of Nazareth is passing by."

38 He cried out, "Jesus, son of David, have mercy on me!" 39 Those who led the way rebuked him, telling him to be quiet; but he cried out all the more, "Son of David, have mercy on me!"

⁴⁰ Jesus stopped and commanded him to be brought to him. When he had come near, he asked him, ⁴¹ "What do you want me to do for you?"

He said, "Lord, that I may see again."

⁴² Jesus said to him, "Receive your sight. Your faith has healed you."

⁴³ Immediately he received his sight and followed him, glorifying God. All the people, when they saw it, praised God.

EXPLORE

I love this man's story. He knew what he wanted, he knew who could get it for him, and he just went for it!

In his era, physical disability was the ticket to a life of poverty and disadvantage (verse 35). We don't know how long this man has been blind, but he's obviously had plenty of experience of being sidelined and considered unimportant.

We don't know why the crowd told him to be quiet (verse 39). Perhaps they thought it was undignified; perhaps they thought a man in his lowly social position had no right to push himself forward; perhaps, since some people at that time even believed that illness or disability was a punishment for sin, they thought he was too sinful to be calling on Jesus.

Unbowed by public opinion, he refuses to be silenced (verse 39). This man stands out from the crowd in more ways than one. It's his faith that brings the healing (verse 42), and that faith is in the Son of David (verses 38–39). This was another name for the Jewish Messiah, the Christ.

Jesus' response is virtually a confirmation that the blind man's title for him is correct. A destitute outsider can see what the religious elite cannot. Despite all their education and privilege, they are spiritually blind, and have failed to see who Jesus is.

The man shows his understanding of the healing by his response. He follows Jesus and gives glory to God (verse 43).

Don't let anything hold you back from following Jesus. Don't worry what anyone else will think. Just call out to Jesus.

ELSEWHERE IN THE BIBLE

> You, God, are my God, earnestly I seek you; I thirst for you, my whole being longs for you, in a dry and parched land where there is no water.
>
> — PSALM 63:1 (NIV)

> "For I know the plans I have for you," declares the LORD, "plans to prosper you and not to harm you, plans to give you hope and a future. Then you will call on me and come and pray to me, and I will listen to you. You will seek me and find me when you seek me with all your heart."
>
> — JEREMIAH 29:11–13 (NIV)

25

DISCOVERING WHAT REALLY MATTERS

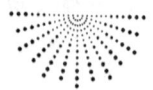

Today we meet another man willing to be undignified in his pursuit of Jesus, but this man is neither powerless nor poor. See what you think of him, and Jesus' reaction to him.

READ LUKE 19:1-10 (WEB)

¹ [Jesus] entered Jericho and was passing through. ² There was a man named Zacchaeus. He was a chief tax collector, and he was rich. ³ He was trying to see who Jesus was, and couldn't because of the crowd, because he was short. ⁴ He ran on ahead, and climbed up into a sycamore tree to see him, for he was going to pass that way.

⁵ When Jesus came to the place, he looked up and saw him, and said to him, "Zacchaeus, hurry and come down, for today I must stay at your house." ⁶ He hurried, came down, and received him joyfully.

⁷ When they saw it, they all murmured, saying, "He has gone to be the guest of a man who is a sinner."

⁸ Zacchaeus stood and said to the Lord, "Behold,

Lord, half of my goods I give to the poor. If I have defrauded anyone of anything, I restore four times as much."

⁹ Jesus said to him, "Today, salvation has come to this house, because he also is a son of Abraham. ¹⁰ For the Son of Man came to seek and to save the lost."

EXPLORE

The story of Zacchaeus gives us a vivid image of God's grace and the strong reactions it provokes.

Confronted by God's generous offer of friendship to Zacchaeus (verse 5), the crowd is annoyed (verse 7). Zacchaeus is basically an organised crime boss (verse 2) who has doubtless made their lives a misery, not only collecting taxes on behalf of their Roman oppressors but inflating the bill for his own financial benefit. It's hard to blame them for thinking there are much nicer people Jesus could have had lunch with.

Zacchaeus responds quite differently. His willingness to abandon his dignity just for a glimpse of the travelling preacher (verse 4) shows that the seed of change has already been sown in his heart. It blossoms into a radical and wholehearted change of life (verse 8) when he looks into Jesus' eyes and sees love and a second chance, rather than condemnation and rejection. He is giving up more than money. He abandons the power his wealth and position has conferred, to seek justice and reparation.

Zacchaeus the crook realizes what Jesus is on about in a way that the pious crowd does not. Jesus didn't come to massage the egos of religious folk, but to turn messy lives around (verse 10). Some of those lives would belong to scoundrels like Zacchaeus; others would be people trapped in more respectable but still pointless existences.

Jesus' whole purpose in coming to earth was to rescue people who know they need it. We can only really know Him, and follow Him, when we grasp that essential fact. Do you need rescuing?

ELSEWHERE IN THE BIBLE

Jesus said:

> "The kingdom of heaven is like a merchant looking for fine pearls. When he found one of great value, he went away and sold everything he had and bought it."
>
> — MATTHEW 13:45–46 (NIV)

26

IDENTITY PARADE

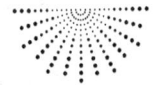

As a small child, I screamed my head off while my mother ran round the house stuffing newspaper into our leaky windows, to "stop the cyclone getting in." I thought the cyclone (hurricane) was a monster coming to attack us. Looking back, there were one or two flaws in both my definition of a cyclone and my faith in the protective properties of paper.

Many people have similar trouble correctly identifying Jesus. Ask Him to help you understand who He is, and why it matters.

READ LUKE 19:35–44 (WEB)

35 Then they brought it [the colt] to Jesus. They threw their cloaks on the colt, and sat Jesus on it. **36** As he went along, they spread their cloaks on the road.

37 As he was now getting near, at the descent of the Mount of Olives, the whole multitude of disciples began to rejoice and praise God with a loud voice for all the mighty works they had seen, **38** saying, "Blessed is the

King who comes in the name of the Lord! Peace in heaven, and glory in the highest!"

39 Some of the Pharisees in the crowd said to him, "Teacher, rebuke your disciples!"

40 He answered them, "I tell you that if they were silent, the stones would cry out."

41 When he came near, he saw the city and wept over it, **42** saying, "If you, even you, had known today the things that make for peace! But now, they are hidden from your eyes. **43** For the days will come upon you, when your enemies will set up a barricade around you, surround you, and hem you in on every side, **44** and will dash you to the ground and your children within you. They will not leave in you one stone on another, because you didn't recognize the time of your visitation."

EXPLORE

Jesus now enters Jerusalem, and the final days of His life. He knows He is heading for execution – the Jewish leaders have put out a warrant for His arrest – but He enters the city anyway.

The colt (verse 35) fulfills a direct prophecy (see the quote from Zechariah below) that would have been well-known to Jesus' Jewish followers. The miracles have shown that Jesus is the Messiah (verse 37), and the colt confirms it.

They fail to recognize, however, that the colt is also a sign He is coming in peace (a king heading into battle would have ridden a warhorse, not a young donkey). Their nationalistic hopes have become tangled in their spiritual hopes. They want the Messiah to get rid of Roman oppression and taxes – a huge issue at the time and yet an underestimation of the purposes of God.

The Pharisees urge Jesus to quieten the crowd (verse 39), perhaps not only because they think it's wrong for Him to be proclaimed Messiah King but because the commotion could draw a backlash from the Roman guards. Jesus replies that what is happening is unstoppable and bigger than they know (verse 40).

The whirlpool of faulty definitions and misunderstandings will reach its tragic culmination several days later when the crowd's joyful cheers turn to ugly shouts of "Crucify him!"

Several decades later, in 70 AD, Jesus' prediction about the destruction of Jerusalem (verses 43–44) will also prove hauntingly accurate. Take careful note that He is not gloating or vengeful over this. He weeps (verse 41), heartbroken that they cannot see Who is with them (verse 44).

There are consequences when we misidentify Jesus. He longs for you to recognize Him as King of the universe, King of the future and the past, because He knows it will transform your daily life and your eternity. Is there anything you would like to say to Him?

ELSEWHERE IN THE BIBLE

This event was predicted 500 years earlier.

> Rejoice greatly, Daughter Zion! Shout, Daughter Jerusalem! See, your king comes to you, righteous and victorious, lowly and riding on a donkey, on a colt, the foal of a donkey. I will take away the chariots from Ephraim and the warhorses from Jerusalem, and the battle bow will be broken. He will proclaim peace to the nations. His rule will

extend from sea to sea and from the [Euphrates] River to the ends of the earth.

— ZECHARIAH 9:9–10 (NIV)

27
APOCALYPSE NOW?

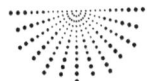

The end of this world is a popular topic for writers and moviemakers and, at the time of writing, world events have led to surging discussions on social media – some tongue-in-cheek, others more genuinely anxious.

Many Christians find it an awkward topic because so many cults have predicted the timing of the end of the world without success that even to raise the subject might draw contempt. But it was a vital topic to Jesus. Ask God to help you understand what He wants to tell you about the future of our planet.

READ LUKE 21:7–8, 10–11, 16–19, 25–28 (WEB)

Jesus told His disciples about the days that were coming.
7 They asked him, "Teacher, when will these things be? What is the sign that these things are about to happen?"

8 He said, "Watch out that you don't get led astray, for many will come in my name, saying, 'I am he,' and, 'The time is at hand.' Don't follow them."

10 Then he said to them, "Nation will rise against

nation, and kingdom against kingdom. ¹¹ There will be great earthquakes, famines, and plagues in various places. There will be terrors and great signs from heaven.

¹⁶ "You will be betrayed even by parents, brothers, relatives, and friends. They will cause some of you to be put to death. ¹⁷ You will be hated by all for my name's sake. ¹⁸ But not a hair of your head will perish. ¹⁹ "By your endurance you will win life.

²⁵ "There will be signs in the sun, moon, and stars; and on the earth distress of nations, in perplexity at the roaring of the sea and the waves; ²⁶ people fainting with fear, and with foreboding of the things which are coming on the world: for the powers of the heavens will be shaken.

²⁷ "Then they will see the Son of Man coming in a cloud with power and great glory. ²⁸ Now when these things begin to happen, look up and lift up your heads, because your redemption is near."

EXPLORE

Some of this reads like the news: war (verse 10), earthquake, drought, fire, famine (leading to empty fields in poor countries, empty supermarkets and soaring costs in rich ones), plague (verse 11), cataclysmic floods, waves and rising sea levels (verse 25).

There are many countries on earth today where being a Christian is illegal and can even be fatal (verse 16) and many more, including my own, where Christianity is increasingly despised (verse 17).

Is the global upheaval we're seeing on our screens the exact one referred to by Jesus in this discussion? It's hard to be sure because such things tend to run in cycles.

However, there are a number of things we can be certain of.

One day, Jesus will return from heaven and the whole earth will see it (verse 27).

Anyone who tries to pin down a date for this is going directly against Jesus' word – verse 8, and explained further in Matthew's Gospel: "No one knows about that day or hour, not even the angels in heaven, nor the Son, but only the Father" (Matthew 24:36 NIV).

It will be a good day for those who know Jesus (verses 18–19,28). It will be a bad day for people who have rejected Jesus (verse 26, see also the extra passage below), and everything evil will be destroyed.

These words from Jesus can be frightening and upsetting. We don't want anyone to be destroyed. Take comfort from the fact that Jesus will look after you – if you ask Him to. You might also pray for family and friends who have not yet understood who Jesus is.

ELSEWHERE IN THE BIBLE

There will be an end and a new beginning.

> "Surely the day is coming; it will burn like a furnace. All the arrogant and every evildoer will be stubble, and the day that is coming will set them on fire," says the LORD Almighty. "Not a root or a branch will be left to them. But for you who revere my name, the sun of righteousness will rise with healing in its rays. And you will go out and frolic like well-fed calves."

— MALACHI 4:1–2 (NIV)

28

THE ORIGINS OF THE COMMUNION SERVICE

I once took part in a communion service in eastern Europe and was overwhelmed by the sensation of being part of one big global family around the table of Jesus, regardless of geography or time zones or cultures. It is an important element of Christian family life, but can seem puzzling initially.

READ LUKE 22:8,13-22 (WEB)

⁸ Jesus sent Peter and John, saying, "Go and prepare the Passover for us, that we may eat it."

He gave them detailed instructions on how to find the right house. ¹³ They went, and found things as Jesus had told them, and they prepared the Passover. ¹⁴ When the hour came, he sat down with the apostles.

¹⁵ He said to them, "I have earnestly desired to eat this Passover with you before I suffer, ¹⁶ for I tell you, I will not eat it again until it is fulfilled in God's Kingdom." ¹⁷ He received the cup, and when he had given thanks, he said, "Take this, and divide it among your-

selves, ⁱ⁸ for I tell you, I will not drink again from the fruit of the vine, until the kingdom of God comes."

¹⁹ He took bread, and when he had given thanks, he broke and gave it to them, saying, "This is my body which is given for you. Do this in memory of me." ²⁰ Likewise, he took the cup after supper, saying, "This cup is the new covenant in my blood, which is poured out for you.

²¹ "But behold, the hand of him who betrays me is with me on the table. ²² The Son of Man will go, as it has been determined, but woe to that man through whom he is betrayed!"

EXPLORE

If you knew you were going to die tomorrow, what would you do tonight? The night before His crucifixion, Jesus gathers His disciples to eat the Passover meal (verse 8), a commemoration of how God had miraculously freed the Jewish people from slavery in Egypt more than a thousand years earlier.

Jesus has some essential things to teach them, and time is running out. He knows that a close friend is about to turn Him in to the religious authorities, with fatal results (verse 21) – but even this is part of the plan (verse 22).

Jesus is about to do something new (verse 20), far beyond the scope of the original Passover, that will bring about the kingdom of God everyone has been waiting for (verse 16). The next agonizing hours will lead to freedom from slavery to sin and death for all of His followers until the end of time.

This meal is famous as the Last Supper, and it is

repeated in Christian churches around the world today according to Jesus' command in verse 19.

To talk of eating Jesus' body (verse 19) and drinking His blood (verse 20) may sound gruesome, but it is not some kind of symbolic cannibalism. It is a sign that we take into our beings the forgiveness Jesus has won for us. It is something that we do together (verse 17) to show that those who believe in Jesus' resurrection and lordship are beneficiaries of the covenant (verse 20) or peace treaty between God and people, effectively signed in his blood.

Communion services vary greatly, from traditional to informal. If you have an opportunity to witness or take part in a communion service, you might like to consider the symbolism behind the words and actions.

ELSEWHERE IN THE BIBLE

> For whenever you eat this bread and drink this cup, you proclaim the Lord's death until he comes.
>
> —1 CORINTHIANS 11:26 (NIV)

29

TRYING AGAIN AFTER DEVASTATING FAILURE

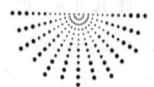

Past mistakes can haunt us, and the fear of failure can stop us going after the things that really matter to us. Jesus has a different view of failure. Open your heart to Him as you read His message today.

READ LUKE 22:31–34, 54–62 (WEB)

During the Passover meal, Jesus said: **31** "Simon, Simon, behold, Satan asked to have you, that he might sift you as wheat, **32** but I prayed for you, that your faith may not fail. And when you have turned again, strengthen your brothers."

33 Peter said to him, "Lord, I am ready to go with you both to prison and to death!"

34 Jesus said, "I tell you, Peter, the rooster will not crow today until you deny three times that you know me."

In the Garden of Gethsemane, Jesus was betrayed. **54** They seized [Jesus], and led him away, and brought him into the high priest's house. Peter followed from a distance. **55** When they had kindled a fire in the middle of the courtyard and had sat down together, Peter sat among them. ⁵⁶ A servant girl saw him as he sat in the light, and looking intently at him, said, "This man also was with him."

⁵⁷ He denied it, saying, "Woman, I don't know him."

⁵⁸ After a little while someone else saw him, and said, "You also are one of them."

But Peter answered, "Man, I am not!"

⁵⁹ After about an hour passed, another confidently affirmed, saying, "Certainly this man also was with him, for he is a Galilean!"

⁶⁰ But Peter said, "Man, I don't know what you are talking about!" Immediately, while he was still speaking, a rooster crowed. ⁶¹ The Lord turned and looked at Peter. Then Peter remembered the Lord's word, how he said to him, "Before the rooster crows today you will deny me three times." ⁶² He went out, and wept bitterly.

EXPLORE

I constantly thank God for the truthfulness of the Bible. Peter became a key leader of the early Christian church. It would have been so easy for the historians to massage the facts a little and make Peter look good. But no, his failure is laid down in stark, uncompromising detail.

At the Last Supper, Peter is full of bravado, so certain that he will go to death and back rather than desert his Lord (verse 33). Just a few short hours later, in the chill early morning after a confusing and frightening night, Peter fails utterly. His piercing grief at his own weakness (verse 62) is something I have identified with a number of times in the course of my Christian life.

The good news for Peter, and for us, is that Jesus did not leave him there in his desolation. After Jesus' resurrection, He restored Peter (see the extra reading below). Just as Peter failed three times, there is a threefold challenge from Jesus. This is not a taunt, but a determination to cut to the heart of the pain and show Peter the way forward. Yes, he has failed, but he is still on the team.

We usually mean well, but sometimes we fail. If God is asking you to face up to failure today, confront it head on, but be gentle with yourself, just as Jesus is. He longs to restore you.

ELSEWHERE IN THE BIBLE

After Jesus' death and resurrection:

> This was now the third time Jesus appeared to his disciples after he was raised from the dead. When they had finished eating, Jesus said to Simon Peter, "Simon son of John, do you love me more than these?"
>
> "Yes, Lord," he said, "you know that I love you."
>
> Jesus said, "Feed my lambs."
>
> *[Jesus asked a second time with the same response, and then...]* The third time he said to him, "Simon son of John, do you love me?"
>
> Peter was hurt because Jesus asked him the third time, "Do you love me?" He said, "Lord, you know all things; you know that I love you."
>
> Jesus said, "Feed my sheep.
>
> — JOHN 21:14–17 (NIV)

30

RIGHT PEOPLE, WRONG REACTION

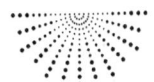

I once failed to recognize a dear friend as she disembarked a plane because she had changed her hairstyle. It was jarring for me to see her looking so different, but we both enjoyed laughing about it.

Lots of people fail to recognize Jesus because He doesn't look how they expect. Unfortunately it's not funny, but deadly serious.

READ LUKE 22:47–48, 66–71; 23:8–11 (WEB)

⁴⁷ While he was still speaking, a crowd came up. Judas, one of the twelve, was leading them. He came near to Jesus to kiss him. ⁴⁸ But Jesus said to him, "Judas, would you betray the Son of Man with a kiss?"

⁶⁶ As soon as it was day, the assembly of the elders of the people were gathered together, both chief priests and scribes, and they led him away into their council, saying, ⁶⁷ "If you are the Christ, tell us."

But he said to them, "If I tell you, you won't believe, ⁶⁸ and if I ask, you will not answer. ⁶⁹ But from now on, the Son of Man will be seated at the right hand of the power of God."

⁷⁰ They all said, "Are you then the Son of God?"

He said to them, "You say that I am."

⁷¹ They said, "Why do we need any more testimony? We have heard it ourselves from his own mouth!"

They took Jesus to the governor, Pilate, who sent him to King Herod... ⁸ Now when Herod saw Jesus, he was exceedingly glad, for he had wanted to see him for a long time, because he had heard many things about him. He hoped to see some miracle done by him. ⁹ He questioned him with many words, but he gave no answers. ¹⁰ The chief priests and the scribes stood there, vehemently accusing him. ¹¹ Herod with his soldiers humiliated him and mocked him. Dressing him in luxurious clothing, they sent him back to Pilate.

EXPLORE

Here we have three totally wrong reactions to Jesus, from people who should have known better.

Judas Iscariot, one of Jesus' inner circle, should have known who Jesus was, but he betrayed Him to the religious leaders for the infamous 30 pieces of silver (verses 47–48). We don't know why he did it, but perhaps he was frustrated by Jesus' failure to generate a military uprising.

The chief priests and scribes (verse 66) were always poring over the Scriptures, and should have picked up on the prophecies that proved who Jesus was. But they were prejudiced against Him from the start, and convinced that He must be lying. They thought they had the evidence to put Him to death (verse 71); they didn't stop to consider that He might actually be telling the truth (verse 70).

King Herod was the Jewish civic leader, who should have had the interests of his people at heart. But he wants to see some magic tricks (verse 8), and when he doesn't get what he wants, like a petulant child he makes fun of the Lord of the Universe and sends Jesus on to His death (verse 11).

Sometimes people say that if they'd lived at the same time as Jesus they wouldn't have so much trouble believing in Him. But the truth is that belief stems from the heart, not the eyes and ears.

Chances are, you're reading this book because you want to know who Jesus is. Ask Him to help you know Him for who He really is. He loves to receive requests like that.

ELSEWHERE IN THE BIBLE

Jesus reaches out to people to save them, and their rejection causes Him profound grief.

> "Jerusalem, Jerusalem, you who kill the prophets and stone those sent to you, how often I have longed to gather your children together, as a hen gathers her chicks under her wings, and you were not willing."
>
> — LUKE 13:34 (NIV)

31

RIGHT REACTION, WRONG PEOPLE

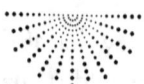

Try to calm the worries in your busy mind as you prepare to read about the death of Jesus.

READ LUKE 23:32–47 (WEB)

³² There were two others, criminals, led out with him to be put to death. ³³ When they came to the place that is called The Skull, they crucified him there with the criminals, one on the right and the other on the left.

³⁴ Jesus said, "Father, forgive them, for they don't know what they are doing."

And they divided his garments among them, by casting lots. ³⁵ The people stood watching. The rulers with them also scoffed at him, saying, "He saved others. Let him save himself, if this is the Christ of God, his chosen one!"

³⁶ The soldiers also mocked him, coming to him and offering him wine vinegar, ³⁷ and saying, "If you are the King of the Jews, save yourself!"

³⁸ An inscription was also written over him: "THIS IS THE KING OF THE JEWS."

⁹⁹ One of the criminals who was hanged insulted him, saying, "Aren't you the Christ? Save yourself and us!" ⁴⁰ But the other rebuked him, saying, "Don't you fear God, seeing you are under the same sentence of condemnation? ⁴¹ And we indeed justly, for we are receiving the due reward for our deeds, but this man has done nothing wrong." ⁴² He said, "Jesus, remember me when you come into your kingdom."

⁴³ Jesus said to him, "Truly I tell you, today you will be with me in paradise."

⁴⁴ It was now about the sixth hour [noon], and darkness came over the whole land until the ninth hour [3pm]. ⁴⁵ The sun was darkened, and the curtain of the temple was torn in two. ⁴⁶ Jesus, calling out with a loud voice, said, "Father, into your hands I commit my spirit!" Having said this, he breathed his last.

⁴⁷ When the centurion saw what had happened, he glorified God, saying, "Certainly this was a righteous man."

EXPLORE

This is the darkest day in the history of the world – even the sun stopped shining (verses 44–45).

As He struggles to draw His last breaths, people are still criticizing Jesus. Their theme is "you saved others so save yourself!" (verses 35,37,39). But the fact is that in order to save others, He had to refuse to save himself. The other "savings" they refer to were temporary – all those people He healed or helped still died eventually.

Someone had to absorb all the poison of several millennia of human rejection of God to provide a way out of eternal death. Jesus is soaking it up into Himself here on the cross.

Only two people come close to understanding that.

The first is a convicted criminal who's done something bad enough to earn the death penalty. He will have no opportunity to make amends for his life choices, but simply because of his expression of faith (verse 42) Jesus tells him He'll see him in heaven later (verse 43).

The second person is a Roman centurion, a Gentile who knows nothing of the Jewish God or the expected Messiah. But as he watches Jesus die, he recognizes something in Jesus that prompts him to praise God (verse 47).

Some find the extent of Jesus' forgiveness offensive, but the good news is that if He could forgive a condemned criminal, He can forgive you and me. Whatever you have done, Jesus' death is enough. You might like to echo the criminal: "Jesus, remember me."

ELSEWHERE IN THE BIBLE

Centuries before Jesus was born, this chillingly accurate prophecy was made:

> All who see me mock me; they hurl insults, shaking their heads. "He trusts in the LORD," they say, "let the LORD rescue him. Let him deliver him, since he delights in him." Dogs surround me, a pack of villains encircles me; they pierce my hands and my feet. All my bones are on display; people stare and gloat over me. They divide my clothes among them and cast lots for my garment.
>
> — PSALM 22:7–8, 16–18 (NIV)

32
ALIVE!

*D*eath is the final frontier. Occasionally, people who have been resuscitated report near-death experiences.

But resurrection is a different matter. Only one man has ever died and returned immortal, never to die again. You might like to ask God to help you understand this most fundamental truth of the Christian faith.

READ LUKE 23:55–24:11 (WEB)

⁵⁵ The women, who had come with him from Galilee, followed, and saw the tomb, and how his body was laid. ⁵⁶ They returned and prepared spices and ointments. On the Sabbath they rested according to the commandment.

24 ¹ But on the first day of the week, at early dawn, they went to the tomb, taking the spices they had prepared. ² They found the stone rolled away from the tomb. ³ They entered in, and did not find the body of the Lord Jesus. ⁴ While they were greatly perplexed about this, behold, two men stood by them in dazzling clothing. ⁵ Becoming terrified, they bowed their faces down to the ground.

The men said to them, "Why do you seek the living among the dead? ⁶ He isn't here, but has risen. Remember how he told you when he was still in Galilee ⁷ that the Son of Man must be delivered into the hands of sinful men and be crucified, and on the third day rise again?"

⁸ They remembered his words, ⁹ and returning from the tomb, they told all these things to the eleven and to all the rest. ¹⁰ It was Mary Magdalene, Joanna, and Mary the mother of James and the other women with them who told these things to the apostles. ¹¹ These words seemed to them to be nonsense, and they didn't believe them.

EXPLORE

These women are at the end of their rope. For three years they have followed an amazing man who seemed to have the answer to the world's problems, only to see Him falsely accused in a kangaroo court, then brutally executed without any resistance.

Imagine the depth of their grief as they approach the tomb to tenderly care for the body of their Lord (verse 1). When they get there, they find that the tomb has apparently been desecrated (verse 2) and the body exhumed without permission (verse 3).

While they are still absorbing this shock, two extremely scary men appear (verse 4) with a very confusing message (verses 5–7). I think by this stage I probably would have just fainted and been done with it.

But thankfully, these women somehow hold it together, and manage to remember and start to unravel the explanations of Jesus that had made no sense at the time (verses 7–8).

When they get back to the others with the astounding good news (verse 9), their story is initially dismissed (verse 11). Tomorrow, we'll see what happens next.

If you find the resurrection hard to get your mind around, don't despair. It seriously messed with the minds of the first witnesses to it. However they came to understand that it was exactly what centuries of Jewish prophets and Jesus himself had said would happen.

ELSEWHERE IN THE BIBLE

Before His death, Jesus had told His disciples:

> "We are going up to Jerusalem, and everything that is written by the prophets about the Son of Man will be fulfilled. He will be delivered over to the Gentiles. They will mock him, insult him and spit on him; they will flog him and kill him. On the third day he will rise again." The disciples did not understand any of this. Its meaning was hidden from them, and they did not know what he was talking about.
>
> — LUKE 18:31–34 (NIV)

33

WITHOUT A DOUBT

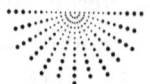

What does the resurrection of Jesus means to you?

READ LUKE 24:36–49, ACTS 1:3 (WEB)

36 As they were talking about these things, Jesus himself stood among them, and said to them, "Peace be with you."

37 But they were terrified and filled with fear, and supposed that they had seen a spirit.

38 He said to them, "Why are you troubled? Why do doubts arise in your hearts? **39** See my hands and my feet, that it is I myself. Touch me and see, for a spirit doesn't have flesh and bones, as you see that I have." **40** When he had said this, he showed them his hands and his feet. **41** While they still didn't believe for joy, and were marveling, he said to them, "Do you have anything here to eat?"

42 They gave him a piece of broiled fish. **43** He took it, and ate it in front of them. **44** He said to them, "This is what I told you, while I was still with you, that everything written about me in the law of Moses, the prophets, and the psalms, must be fulfilled."

45 Then he opened their minds to understand the Scriptures. **46** He said to them, "Thus it is written, that the Christ should suffer and rise from the dead on the third day, **47** and that repentance for the forgiveness of sins should be preached in his name to all nations, beginning at Jerusalem. **48** You are witnesses of these things. **49** Behold, I send out the promise of my Father upon you. But wait in the city until you are clothed with power from on high."

3 He presented himself alive to them after his suffering, by many proofs, appearing to them over a period of forty days, and speaking about the kingdom of God.

EXPLORE

Jesus' disciples knew for a certainty that He was dead. Then several women had come back from the tomb with some wild story that Jesus was alive again, but they had put it down to hysteria. After all, it had been a trying few days for everyone.

Now here He is, standing among them (verse 36).

I think if I had seen a friend die, and three days later he came into the room and started talking to me, I'd be just as scared as these disciples were (verse 37). This is very weird. But Jesus is patient. He knows it will take some time for the truth to sink in.

He graciously invites them to touch and see (verses 39–40) and even offers to eat something (verses 41–43) since that is something a ghost can't do.

But this was not a one-off occurrence that could be passed off as an hallucination from the depths of grief. Jesus continued to prove himself for nearly six weeks, teaching them as He went along (verse 3). He made absolutely certain that they would understand what his death and resurrection were all about. They had to be clear on the facts, because they were to be the historic witnesses (verse 48), empowered by God (verse 49).

The resurrection is not an optional extra. Without it, Christianity is nothing more than a moral code. Death and separation from God was the consequence of human sin, and in dying, Jesus shouldered that consequence for every person who belongs to Him. In His resurrection, He has beaten death. Because He rose, we too can have eternal life.

If you have doubts, take them honestly to God. He can cope. But be assured that this is history, not fantasy.

ELSEWHERE IN THE BIBLE

> If you declare with your mouth, "Jesus is Lord," and believe in your heart that God raised him from the dead, you will be saved.
>
> — ROMANS 10:9 (NIV)

34
WAITING

Waiting can be one of the hardest things to do, but it can also be a special time of anticipation – a pregnant woman waiting for her baby, a child waiting for Christmas, a couple waiting for their wedding day.

The disciples are waiting for their lives to be turned upside down.

READ ACTS 1:4–11 (WEB)

4 And while staying with them, [Jesus] commanded them, "Don't depart from Jerusalem, but wait for the promise of the Father, which you heard from me. 5 For John baptized with water, but you will be baptized with the Holy Spirit not many days from now."

6 Therefore when they had come together, they asked him, "Lord, are you now restoring the kingdom to Israel?"

7 He said to them, "It is not for you to know times or seasons which the Father has set by his own authority. 8 But you will receive power when the Holy Spirit has

come upon you. You will be my witnesses in Jerusalem, in all Judea and Samaria, and to the ends of the earth."

⁹ When he had said these things, as they were looking on, he was taken up, and a cloud hid him from their sight. ¹⁰ While they were looking steadfastly into the sky as he went, behold, two men stood by them in white clothing, ¹¹ and said, "Men of Galilee, why do you stand looking into the sky? This Jesus, who was taken up from you into heaven, will come back in the same way as you saw him go into heaven."

EXPLORE

Numerous times before His death, Jesus discussed with His disciples the fact that He would have to go away, but that He would leave someone else in His place to look after them. He meant the Holy Spirit (verse 5). They still don't really understand what that means, but they will soon.

The disciples also haven't yet understood that the goal is not political freedom (verse 6). Jesus tells them to leave that up to God (verse 7), and firmly changes their focus.

Much more than the future of Israel is at stake. The Holy Spirit will empower them to testify about Jesus, not just to Jews (Jerusalem and Judea), but to Samaria (a despised neighbor) and the whole world (verse 8).

Jesus is then taken up into "heaven." We don't know the geography of heaven, but we do know that it is where God's powerful presence is clearly visible. We know that Jesus is representing us before God, a little like a lawyer advocating on our behalf. We also know that Jesus is coming back (verse 11).

God the Father, Jesus the Son, and the Holy Spirit

are three different persons, but somehow all the one God. This is one of the great mysteries of the Christian faith.

The life, death and resurrection of Jesus Christ is good news designed to be shared. Will you share it?

ELSEWHERE IN THE BIBLE

After He rose from the dead, Jesus gave a command to His disciples:

> "All authority in heaven and on earth has been given to me. Therefore go and make disciples of all nations, baptizing them in the name of the Father and of the Son and of the Holy Spirit, and teaching them to obey everything I have commanded you. And surely I am with you always, to the very end of the age."
>
> — MATTHEW 28:18–20 (NIV)

35
A SPIRITUAL TURNING POINT

There have been times when I have felt shy and reluctant to talk about my relationship with God. But there have been times when the words have just poured out of my mouth, with a passion and clarity that astonishes me. That is the kind of thing the Holy Spirit does, when we let Him. Ask God to help you understand what His Holy Spirit wants to do in your life.

READ ACTS 2:1–13 (WEB)

¹ When the day of Pentecost had come, they were all together in one place. ² Suddenly there came from heaven a sound like the rushing of a mighty wind, and it filled all the house where they were sitting. ³ Tongues like fire appeared and were distributed to them, and one sat on each of them. ⁴ They were all filled with the Holy Spirit, and began to speak with other languages, as the Spirit gave them the ability to speak.

⁵ Now there were dwelling in Jerusalem Jews, devout men from every nation under heaven. ⁶ At this sound,

the multitude came together and were bewildered, because each one heard them speaking in his own language. ⁷ They were all amazed and marveled, saying to one another, "Aren't all these who are speaking Galileans? ⁸ How do we hear, each of us in our own native language? ⁹ Parthians, Medes, Elamites, and people from Mesopotamia, Judea, Cappadocia, Pontus, Asia, ¹⁰ Phrygia, Pamphylia, Egypt, the parts of Libya around Cyrene, visitors from Rome, both Jews and proselytes, ¹¹ Cretans and Arabians: we hear them telling in our own languages the mighty works of God!"

¹² They were all amazed, and were perplexed, saying to one another, "What does this mean?" ¹³ Others, mocking, said, "They are filled with new wine."

EXPLORE

Pentecost (verse 1) was a Jewish festival marking 50 days after the Passover festival, but it has become part of the Christian vocabulary because of what happened that first Pentecost after Jesus' death and resurrection.

This is a turning point in world history. Before this, people with a special role to fulfill for God would be empowered by His Spirit for that particular task, but now, all Christians are indwelt by the Holy Spirit, all the time.

This doesn't mean God "operates" us like remote-control puppets. Our spirit and the Holy Spirit dwell side by side, and He will not force His will on us.

But we can hand over our lives to God, asking Him to guide us by His Spirit and allow us to be part of His purposes for the world.

The outcome, on this inaugural occasion, was that Jesus' followers spoke in languages they had never learned. A bunch of country boys from Galilee (verse 7) suddenly poured forth every cosmopolitan language imaginable (verses 9–10). The result? The audience heard about the wonders of God (verse 11). From this day forward, everyone baptized in the name of Jesus receives the Holy Spirit.

If you are a Christian, the Holy Spirit lives in you and, if you let Him, will empower you to declare the wonders of God. Just as some people ridiculed the disciples and said they were drunk (verse 13), people will sometimes laugh at your words and beliefs. However, others are waiting eagerly to hear about it.

ELSEWHERE IN THE BIBLE

Centuries before, God said:

> "And afterward, I will pour out my Spirit on all people. Your sons and daughters will prophesy, your old men will dream dreams, your young men will see visions. Even on my servants, both men and women, I will pour out my Spirit in those days. And everyone who calls on the name of the Lord will be saved."
>
> — JOEL 2:28–29,32 (NIV)

36

WOUNDED BY OUR OWN SINS

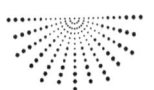

Sometimes our mistakes can be heartbreaking – for ourselves as well as others. Jesus offers a fresh start.

READ ACTS 2:22–24, 32, 36–42 (WEB)

After the coming of the Holy Spirit, Peter stood up and spoke. **22** "Men of Israel, hear these words! Jesus of Nazareth, a man attested by God to you by mighty works and wonders and signs which God did by him among you, as you yourselves know, **23** this man delivered up by the deliberate plan and foreknowledge of God, you have taken by the hand of lawless men, crucified and killed. **24** God raised him up, having freed him from the agony of death, because it was not possible that he should be held by it.

32 "This Jesus God raised up, and of that we all are witnesses.

36 "Let all the house of Israel therefore know for certain that God has made him both Lord and Christ, this Jesus whom you crucified."

37 Now when they heard this, they were cut to the heart, and said to Peter and the rest of the apostles, "Brothers, what shall we do?"

38 Peter said to them, "Repent, and be baptized, every one of you, in the name of Jesus Christ for the forgiveness of your sins, and you will receive the gift of the Holy Spirit. **39** For the promise is for you, and for your children, and for all who are far off, as many as the Lord our God will call to himself."

40 With many other words he testified, and exhorted them, saying, "Save yourselves from this crooked generation!"

41 Then those who gladly received his word were baptized. There were added that day about three thousand souls. **42** They devoted themselves to the apostles' teaching and fellowship, to the breaking of bread, and prayer.

EXPLORE

This powerful sermon from Peter follows immediately after the disciples' fiery experience of the Holy Spirit that we read about yesterday. That extraordinary display of linguistics has created a captive audience.

The teaching of Jesus in the weeks after His resurrection now stands Peter in good stead. He explains various Bible predictions, and the way Jesus fulfills them (if you have a Bible you can read them in the full text of this chapter of Acts).

He is adamant that death could not keep Jesus in its clutches (verses 24,32), because Jesus is the Lord of life (verse 36). He is clear that the execution of Jesus was not a violation of God's plan, but the fulfillment of it (verse 23). This does not make the people any less responsible for Jesus' death (verses 23,36).

When the people hear that they have participated in the murder of the one they had waited so long to see, it strikes them like a physical agony (verse 37). They want to make up for what they've done, but what can they possibly do?

The startling answer is not a pronouncement of punishment, but the offer of a new life, in intimate relationship with God (verse 38). Three thousand people responded immediately and were baptized, but it wasn't a shallow response soon forgotten. It changed the whole structure of their lives (verse 42).

Jesus died for you. He invites you to turn to Him – to ask Him to turn your life around.

ELSEWHERE IN THE BIBLE

Jesus said:

> "For God so loved the world that he gave his one and only Son, that whoever believes in him shall not perish but have eternal life. For God did not send his Son into the world to condemn the world, but to save the world through him."
>
> — JOHN 3:16–17 (NIV)

37
EVERYONE MATTERS

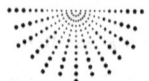

A friend of mine lost two of her toes in an accident and found it hard to balance. They were such tiny body parts, ones that people rarely notice, but they were important.

The church of Jesus is like a body. He is the head, controlling where we go and why, and we are all the other bits, with different roles and responsibilities. When every part is working well, it hums. When any part suffers, all of it feels the impact.

READ ACTS 2:42–47 (WEB)

⁴² They devoted themselves to the apostles' teaching and fellowship, to the breaking of bread, and prayer. ⁴³ Awe came upon every soul, and many wonders and signs were being done through the apostles. ⁴⁴ All who believed were together, and had all things in common. ⁴⁵ They were selling their possessions and goods, and distributing the proceeds to all, as anyone had need. ⁴⁶ Day by day, continuing steadfastly together in the temple, and breaking bread in their homes, they took

their food with gladness and singleness of heart, ⁴⁷ praising God, and having favor with all the people. The Lord added to their number day by day those who were being saved.

EXPLORE

This is "church in action." A church is not a building, or even an organization. It is a family of believers. Relationship with God brings relationship with His people. We all need each other if we are going to function correctly.

Christians today differ as to whether they choose to live together in the type of commune described here (verses 44–45) though it clearly strengthened the fledgling church at the time it was forming and bolstered it against intense persecution to come. It is a description rather than a command, so if any church tries to force this lifestyle upon you, take a step back. Likewise, putting the pressing needs of others before our own creature comforts is a godly principle, but financial gifts to the church should be voluntary and from the heart, not forced or shamed.

Hearing the apostles' teaching (verse 42) through reading the Bible and having it explained in sermons and Bible studies will help us grow in confidence and understanding of our faith.

Christians are called to: meet together for encouragement and growth, and fellowship with each other over meals (verse 46); give praise to God; be good citizens (verse 47); obey Jesus' command to reach out to people who don't yet know Him (verse 47).

If you choose to follow Jesus, you will need the love and support of other Christians, and they will need your love and support. Begin looking for a local church fellowship, and in the meantime there are also online options.

ELSEWHERE IN THE BIBLE

> Let us hold unswervingly to the hope we profess, for he who promised is faithful. And let us consider how we may spur one another on toward love and good deeds, not giving up meeting together, as some are in the habit of doing, but encouraging one another—and all the more as you see the Day approaching.
>
> — HEBREWS 10:23–25 (NIV)

The Bible also describes a good church leader.

> Be shepherds of God's flock that is under your care, watching over them—not because you must, but because you are willing, as God wants you to be; not pursuing dishonest gain, but eager to serve; not lording it over those entrusted to you, but being examples to the flock.
>
> — 1 PETER 5:2–3 (NIV)

38
BOLDLY GO

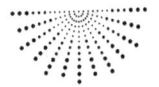

*A*sk God to give you the courage to be His person in a world that is hostile to faith.

READ ACTS 4:10–13, 19–20, 24–31 (WEB)

Peter and John were jailed after healing a disabled man in the name of Jesus. The next day, the religious authorities gathered to question them, and, filled with the Holy Spirit, Peter replied: **10** "May it be known to you all, and to all the people of Israel, that in the name of Jesus Christ of Nazareth, whom you crucified, whom God raised from the dead, this man stands here before you healed. **11** [Jesus] is 'the stone that was rejected by you, the builders, which has become the cornerstone.' **12** There is salvation in no one else, for there is no other name under heaven that is given among men, by which we must be saved!"

13 Now when they saw the boldness of Peter and John, and perceived that they were uneducated and ordinary men, they marveled. They recognized that they had been with Jesus.

They commanded them not to teach in the name of Jesus. ¹⁹ But Peter and John answered them, "Whether it is right in the sight of God to listen to you rather than to God, judge for yourselves, ²⁰ for we can't help telling of the things we saw and heard."

Peter and John went back to the other believers and told them what had happened. ²⁴ When they heard it, they lifted up their voices together to God, and said, "Sovereign Lord, who made the heaven, the earth, the sea, and all that is in them; ²⁵ who by the mouth of your servant, David, said by the Holy Spirit,

'Why do the nations rage, and the peoples plot in vain? ²⁶ The kings of the earth take a stand, and the rulers take council together, against the Lord, and against his anointed one.'

²⁷ "For truly in this city, both Herod and Pontius Pilate, with the Gentiles and the people of Israel, were gathered together against your holy servant, Jesus, whom you anointed, ²⁸ to do whatever your hand and your plan had predestined to happen. ²⁹ Now, Lord, look at their threats, and grant to your servants to speak your word with all boldness, ³⁰ while you stretch out your hand to heal; and signs and wonders are performed through the name of your holy Servant Jesus."

³¹ When they had prayed, the place was shaken where they were gathered together. They were all filled with the Holy Spirit, and they spoke the word of God with boldness.

EXPLORE

Can this be the same Peter who shrank in fear on the night of Jesus' betrayal?

Since then, he has met the resurrected Jesus and

received reinstatement and deep further teaching from Him. Peter has also received the extraordinary gift of the Holy Spirit living inside him.

This time, Peter is not isolated or alone – his colleague John stands beside him. Peter and John are firm on the facts of their faith (verse 10). They might not be academics (very 13) but they know the Bible well enough to quote it back to professional Bible teachers (verse 11).

Jesus' promise that the Holy Spirit will give them "words and wisdom" (see extra passage below) is abundantly fulfilled – especially in their unflinching challenge to these powerful men in verses 19 and 20.

Hearing the news, the Christian community prays for courage under fire, reminding themselves of God's bigness (verse 24) and His unassailable plan (verse 28). Their lives are in danger, but instead of asking for safety they pray for boldness to speak the truth all the more (verse 28)!

Their example teaches us how to face up to opposition to our faith: keep the company of other Christians, know our Bibles, pray hard, remember who God is, and trust Him for the right words at the right time.

Peter became a key leader in the early Christian church, and we can read some of his letters that have been recorded in the New Testament. He was still very human, and made other mistakes in the course of his life. But in the power of the Holy Spirit he could do remarkable things for God. So can we.

ELSEWHERE IN THE BIBLE

Jesus told His disciples:

> "But before all this, they will seize you and persecute you. They will hand you over to synagogues and put you in prison, and you will be brought before kings and governors, and all on account of my name. And so you will bear testimony to me.
>
> "But make up your mind not to worry beforehand how you will defend yourselves. For I will give you words and wisdom that none of your adversaries will be able to resist or contradict."

— LUKE 21:12–15 (NIV)

39

THE DAMASCUS ROAD

*D*o you ever wonder where your life is headed? Ask God if He has a purpose for you.

READ ACTS 9:3–9,15–20 (WEB)

A man named Saul set out to arrest believers on behalf of the Jewish leaders. ³ As he traveled, he got close to Damascus, and suddenly a light from heaven shone around him. ⁴ He fell to the ground, and heard a voice saying to him, "Saul, Saul, why do you persecute me?"

⁵ He said, "Who are you, Lord?"

And he said, "I am Jesus, whom you are persecuting. ⁶ But rise and enter into the city, and you will be told what you must do."

⁷ The men traveling with him stood speechless, hearing the sound, but seeing no one. ⁸ Saul rose from the ground, but when his eyes were opened, he saw no one. So they led him by the hand, and brought him into Damascus. ⁹ He was without sight for three days, and neither ate nor drank.

God told a believer named Ananias to go and heal

Saul, but Ananias was afraid. **15** But the Lord said to him, "Go, for he is my chosen instrument to bear my name before the Gentiles and kings, and the children of Israel. **16** For I will show him how many things he must suffer for the sake of my name."

17 Ananias departed and entered the house. Laying his hands on him, he said, "Brother Saul, the Lord Jesus who appeared to you on the road by which you came, has sent me that you may regain your sight and be filled with the Holy Spirit."

18 Immediately something like scales fell from his eyes, and he regained his sight. He rose and was baptized. **19** He took food and was strengthened.

Saul stayed several days with the disciples who were at Damascus. **20** Immediately in the synagogues he proclaimed Jesus, that he is the Son of God.

EXPLORE

If you've ever heard anyone refer to a "Damascus Road experience," this is the original. It is a total change of life direction for a brilliant young Pharisee and religious expert named Saul. History knows him better by his other name, Paul.

There are two examples of fear in this story, and two corresponding examples of Spirit-empowered boldness.

Paul fell to the ground in terror when the light from heaven flashed around him (verse 4). Ananias's knees went weak when God told him to help the infamous man who had been throwing Christians into prison.

Ananias believed God and went boldly into the lion's den (verse 17) even daring to call this fearsome man "brother." Paul went straight out and began vigorously expounding the very religion he had so brutally tried to stop (verse 20).

Both of them acted from their conviction that Jesus was Lord of all creation, the Son of God (verses 5,20).

I wonder what Paul's thoughts were in those three days of darkness (verse 9) as he waited to see what would become of him (verse 6). Instead of punishment, God sent healing and the gift of His Holy Spirit (verse 17).

This vicious opponent of the faith turned out to be God's secret weapon, taking the good news of Jesus to non-Jews (verse 15). Paul used his education to good effect, and even today his many letters recorded in the New Testament help us to understand our faith.

Grace is an "undeserved free gift," and that's what Paul received from Ananias and from God. You and I can receive that same grace of God. Reach out for it. If you already have, praise God for His generosity.

ELSEWHERE IN THE BIBLE

In later years, Paul wrote:

> This righteousness is given through faith in Jesus Christ to all who believe ... for all have sinned and fall short of the glory of God, and all are justified freely by his grace through the redemption that came by Christ Jesus.
>
> — ROMANS 3:22–24 (NIV)

40
EARTH SHATTERING

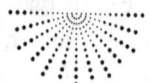

This is the last of the forty Bible readings in our book. Following Jesus will shake your life to its foundations. Are you ready for that?

READ ACTS 16:25–34 (WEB)

In the city of Philippi, Paul and Silas cast a spirit out of a slave girl who had earned money for her owners by telling fortunes. A side-effect was that she couldn't tell fortunes anymore! In the ruckus that followed, they were flogged and thrown in jail. ²⁵ About midnight Paul and Silas were praying and singing hymns to God, and the prisoners were listening to them. ²⁶ Suddenly there was a great earthquake, so that the foundations of the prison were shaken; and immediately all the doors were opened, and everyone's bonds came loose.

²⁷ The jailer woke up, and seeing the prison doors open, drew his sword and was about to kill himself, supposing that the prisoners had escaped. ²⁸ But Paul cried with a loud voice, "Don't harm yourself, for we are all here!"

29 The jailer called for lights, rushed in, and fell down trembling before Paul and Silas. **30** He brought them out, and said, "Sirs, what must I do to be saved?"

31 They said, "Believe in the Lord Jesus, and you will be saved, you and your household." **32** They spoke the word of the Lord to him, and to all who were in his house.

33 He took them the same hour of the night and washed their wounds, and was immediately baptized, he and all his household. **34** He brought them up into his house, and set food before them, and rejoiced greatly, with all his household, that he had believed in God.

EXPLORE

Skeptics would say this earthquake was a coincidence, but as an African bishop once said, "When I pray, coincidences happen." Judging by the jailer's reaction (verse 30), it was crystal clear to him that the spiritual noises he'd been hearing (verse 25) were directly linked with the movement of the earth. Paul and Silas's refusal to dodge the legal ramifications of what they'd been doing also made an impression (verse 28).

A seismic event occurred that night in the jailer's own life and that of all his family (verse 33).

Not everybody becomes a Christian the instant they hear about Jesus. For some it is a slow process of inquiry and evaluation, but there comes a moment when we just have to acknowledge that we want to be saved, and Jesus is the answer.

If you've been weighing everything up as you've read this book, but you now find the evidence for Christianity compelling, don't sit on the fence any longer.

Seize hold of Jesus and the rescue He offers you. Believe in Him and be baptized.

If you're still uncertain, keep on asking questions, going to a church, and seriously seeking the God of the universe – don't let anything deter you from your quest.

If you already belong to Jesus, keep on getting to know Him better, but also be brave in taking the message of Jesus to your friends and your household. Like the jailer in today's story, you've discovered overwhelming joy. Tell the people you love.

ELSEWHERE IN THE BIBLE

Jesus said:

> "My sheep listen to my voice; I know them, and they follow me. I give them eternal life, and they shall never perish; no one will snatch them out of my hand. My Father, who has given them to me, is greater than all; no one can snatch them out of my Father's hand. I and the Father are one."
>
> — JOHN 10:27–30 (NIV)

WHERE TO NEXT?

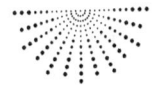

What have you decided about Jesus? If you are still unsure, may I encourage you to keep exploring, and keep praying something like this: God, if you exist, show me the truth of Jesus Christ, and show me why it matters.

If you have chosen to belong to Jesus, welcome to the Christian family.

THE CHRISTIAN FAMILY

We might live in different countries and speak different languages or dialects, but we are all one family, with God as loving heavenly Father.

I continually discover that I can meet a Christian for the first time who might be from a different background and culture to me, and we have an instant bond. I have friends who do not share my faith, and they are dear to me, but this particular connection is unique to my friendships with Christians.

Develop your family relationships by spending time with other family members. Become part of a church fellowship, both for the support and encouragement they will give you, and for the support and encouragement you can give them. If you don't yet know which church to attend, try searching online for churches near you, and ask God to help you find one that is true to biblical priorities. (None will be perfect, because they are full of human beings.)

Develop your relationship with your heavenly Father, by spending time with Him. Make a habit of prayer, both talking and listening. You won't always know what to say and how to say it. But it will gradually become more natural for you to talk to Him about all sorts of things.

Keep on reading the Bible, God's major form of communication with you. Lots of Christians find it helps anchor them if they spend a little time reading it each day.

TWO USEFUL RESOURCES TO GET YOU STARTED

Scripture Union, the British publisher who published the original version of *Meet the Real Jesus*, have various resources available in print or online to help you understand and engage with the Bible. Find them at https://content.scriptureunion.org.uk/bible-reading-guides

Michael Youssef at Leading the Way is pastor of a church in the USA who provides reliable and engaging Bible teaching online, on television, and through apps. Find him at https://ltw.org/

PRAYER: CONVERSATION WITH GOD

The basis of all relationships, including relationship with God, is communication. Prayer enables humans to communicate with God. May I encourage you to explore honest prayer and develop a habit of communication?

Many Christians have found it refreshing and spiritually nourishing to talk to God about all sorts of things. It might seem a little awkward at first – a bit like when you begin chatting with a new acquaintance – but as you get to know God better it will become more natural, and a very special part of your life.

TYPES OF PRAYER

There are all kinds of prayers in the Bible. People begged and pleaded with God, people shouted at God in anger or frustration, people urged God with great passion, people simply adored God in wonder and praise. You can be absolutely honest; God can take it.

Prayer doesn't need special words or formulas. Just talk to God the way you normally talk. He loves to hear from you. Tell Him what you think of Him, what is happening for you, ask Him to take some action in your life or the lives of others or to help you understand something, or just enjoy His presence. Nothing is too big or too small for God – you can pray for world peace or a school exam.

Pray with respect because God is the Lord of the universe, but also pray with trust and confidence, because He is your loving heavenly Father. You can be confident that He will listen to you.

You can pray with a group of people, or alone. You can say the words out loud, or silently inside your head. When you become a Christian, God's Holy Spirit actually lives inside you, so you can talk to God at any hour of the day or night, and He will hear you. Sometimes you won't be able to find the words to say, and then God steps in.

> ... the Spirit helps us in our weakness. We do not know what we ought to pray for, but the Spirit himself intercedes for us through wordless groans.
>
> — ROMANS 8:26 (NIV)

IN JESUS' NAME

You might hear Christians finish a prayer by saying "in Jesus' name. Amen." On the night before He died, Jesus comforted his disciples with a series of deep teachings, including this promise.

> ... I will do whatever you ask in my name, so that the Father may be glorified in the

Son. You may ask me for anything in my name, and I will do it.

— JOHN 14:13–14 (NIV)

Note that it's not some kind of lucky charm, but a submission to God's will with a focus on God's glory.

A TWO-WAY CONVERSATION

Prayer includes listening.

People might say "God told me…" This doesn't usually mean they heard an audible voice saying specific words, although sometimes people do hear a voice or see a vision of Jesus speaking to them.

Often it means that as they read the Bible, they are aware of God speaking to them about a specific situation, through the words written there. Sometimes it means that after much prayer they have become convinced God wants them to take a certain course of action, because their Bible readings, the advice they receive from godly friends, and the events taking place in their lives all seem to be pointing in one direction.

Beware also that occasionally people say "God told me…" because they want you to do as they say! If someone says they have a message from God for you, feel free to test it by seeing what the Bible has to say, talking to God about it yourself, and discussing it with a trusted Christian leader.

THE LORD'S PRAYER

We have already encountered the prayer Jesus taught his disciples in Luke 11. Below is the version in traditional language based on the King James Version of the Bible. This prayer is not meant to be recited mindlessly. It provides a model of the types of things we are encouraged to talk to God about.

> Our Father, who art in heaven,
> Hallowed be thy Name.
> Thy Kingdom come.
> Thy will be done on earth as it is in heaven.
> Give us this day our daily bread.
> And forgive us our trespasses,
> As we forgive those who trespass against us.
> And lead us not into temptation,
> But deliver us from evil.
> For thine is the kingdom,
> The power, and the glory,
> For ever and ever. Amen.

WHY READING THE BIBLE HELPS

The Bible is central to the Christian faith, not because the letters on the page are somehow magical, but because God's Holy Spirit speaks to His people through it.

Even though it was written thousands of years ago, the Bible is not a "dead" book. Daily life has changed dramatically, but human nature hasn't changed, and God's nature hasn't changed. In the Bible, God has something to say to you that is relevant to everything you will ever face in your life.

It has been described as a handbook for living, an owner's manual, and a love letter from God to the humans He created. It is the record of His design for human life. It is a living message from God to you.

WHAT'S IN IT?

The Bible is a library of 66 books by different authors, written between about 2000 BC and AD 100.

The first 39 books, Genesis to Malachi, make up the

Old Testament. (These writings also comprise the Jewish Bible.) This section contains history, poetry and prophecy, telling the story of God's relationship with the Jewish people. Jewish history looks forward to the coming of a Messiah, a rescuer to save the people from oppression and their disconnection from God.

Christianity identifies Jesus Christ as the fulfillment of that prediction. Christ is not Jesus' surname – it is the Greek translation of the Hebrew word Messiah. Jesus described himself as being that person the Jewish people had been awaiting for so long.

The other 27 books, the New Testament, were written after Jesus came. They contain the four biographies of Jesus already mentioned, a history of the beginnings of the Christian church, and correspondence from early Christian leaders about important issues of faith.

Despite this diversity, it hangs together as one book – God's Word.

CAN I TRUST THE BIBLE?

Scholars who study ancient texts of any kind say that the more copies you have of a text, and the older they are, the more certain you can be that what you are reading is what was originally written. There are enormous numbers of ancient copies of the Bible text, all written painstakingly by hand. There are only very minor variations between all the copies, and none of the differences threatens any major point of Christian doctrine. It is the most trustworthy ancient document available in the modern world.

Archeologists, literary scholars and theologians have spent countless hours poring over the Bible, and they have made their findings widely available.

These are some of the things that the Bible says about itself:

> All Scripture is God-breathed and is useful for teaching, rebuking, correcting and training in righteousness, so that the servant of God may be thoroughly equipped for every good work.
>
> — 2 TIMOTHY 3:16–17 (NIV)

> Above all, you must understand that no prophecy of Scripture came about by the prophet's own interpretation of things. For prophecy never had its origin in the human will, but prophets, though human, spoke from God as they were carried along by the Holy Spirit.
>
> — 2 PETER 1:20–21 (NIV)

> For the word of God is alive and active. Sharper than any double-edged sword, it penetrates even to dividing soul and spirit, joints and marrow; it judges the thoughts and attitudes of the heart.
>
> — HEBREWS 4:12 (NIV)

I acknowledge that these statements above are circular – the Bible is saying it about itself. But I also invite you to open your mind to the possibility that these statements are true, and useful for you.

If you'd like to probe more deeply into the reliability

of the Bible and the historical evidence for Jesus, I recommend *Is Jesus History?* by John Dickson. It is a short and readable book that tackles a lot of the questions you might very naturally have, in an honest and forthright way, giving you the freedom to make up your own mind.

Ultimately, my own reliance on the Bible stems from Jesus' attitude to it. He quoted it constantly, taught from it, and treated it as authoritative for human life.

HOW DO I USE IT?

If the Bible is God's message, we can't pick and choose which bits we're going to accept and which to ignore. The parts we don't like need to be wrestled with rather than discarded.

One way in which we can understand it more clearly is to read it in the context of other parts of the Bible, the cultural understandings of a given period, and the purpose of the writing. For example, when the Bible says, "In the heavens God has pitched a tent for the sun. It is like a bridegroom coming out of his chamber, like a champion rejoicing to run his course" (Psalm 19:4–5 NIV), it is being poetic about the beauty of creation and the power of God, not making a scientific statement about our solar system.

Similarly, we shouldn't be grabbing verses in isolation and bending them to suit our will.

Please be aware that many of the people who quote the Bible in the media to show that the Bible can't be trusted are not people who want to learn from the Bible or who have studied the Bible. They are grabbing random quotes out of context with the purpose of shocking their listeners.

Don't take my word for it either. Read the Bible for yourself, fully and in context, and make up your own mind.

WHAT CHRISTIANITY IS AND ISN'T

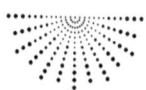

Christianity is not a code of conduct or a social movement or even a charitable cause. It is much more than a hobby or interest. It shapes the fundamental direction of a person's life towards building loving relationships with God and His people and pursuing God's will ahead of our own.

WHAT HAPPENED TO THE WORLD?

As discussed previously, Christian beliefs are drawn from the Bible because it is where God has chosen to record His design for humanity.

The Bible says the first humans enjoyed perfect relationship with God, with each other, and with the planet: "God saw all that he had made, and it was very good" (Genesis 1:31 NIV).

The first humans were given free will; God wanted genuine relationships with his people, not a puppet show. However, these people veered into expressing their free will not by serving their loving Father-God but by rebellion – wanting power, wanting to control their own lives.

At heart, they wanted to make their own gods, and this is what the Bible calls "sin." Individual sins, the fiery darts that cause suffering, might take many different shapes, but their common denominator is that we worship something other than God... other people, our family, human ingenuity, our own opinions, the creation instead of the Creator, and so on.

Everything was ruined by this upending of God's design. It was as though the very DNA of Earth fractured.

Death became part of the human experience for the first time. Every relationship was mangled. People feared and ignored God. People hated and killed and suspected each other. The planet, designed to give food and enjoyment, gave struggle and disaster instead.

This broken, messed-up world was fit only to be demolished. The human race and the planet were put on death row.

WHAT DID GOD DO ABOUT IT?

The story of humanity could have ended there, but God still loved the people He'd made so much that He launched a rescue mission. However, the mess couldn't just be ignored or somehow resolve itself – the death penalty had to be served. Sin had very serious consequences.

That's where Jesus comes in. Jesus was both God and human, in the one person. He was the only sinless human who ever lived – the only one who didn't deserve to be on death row.

> For we do not have a high priest who is unable to empathize with our weaknesses, but we have one who has been tempted in every way, just as we are—yet he did not sin.
>
> — HEBREWS 4:15 (NIV)

He volunteered to take our death sentence, absorbing millennia of evil into himself on the cross, so we could be released from prison.

> For God so loved the world that he gave his one and only Son, that whoever believes in him shall not perish but have eternal life.
>
> — JOHN 3:16–17 (NIV)

IS EVERYTHING OKAY, THEN?

Because of Jesus' perfection and divinity, His one death was enough to bear the death penalty for every human who ever lived. Everyone. Even the worst people you can imagine.

But we have to want it. Not everyone will choose Jesus. Some will prefer it on death row – maybe it's where all their friends are, or they prefer to keep looking for some other way out, or they just want to continue to be gods.

But Jesus said there is no other solution. The only way out is full pardon, through taking hold of Jesus' death in our place.

> "I am the way and the truth and the life. No

one comes to the Father except through me."

— JOHN 14:6 (NIV)

God yearns for every human to take advantage of His rescue plan, but He won't force us to do so, because that would be a fundamental violation of relationship. Love must be voluntary, or it's not love. One of God's gifts to humankind is the freedom to choose Him or not choose Him.

WHAT ABOUT YOU?

If you haven't yet chosen Jesus, but you're fed up with life on death row and you want to change sides, it's remarkably simple. You just have to tell God, in ordinary words. You may like to pray this little prayer or something similar, which you can say out loud or in your head:

> Dear God, I'm sorry that I've been part of the problem and have rebelled against You, trying to take control and be my own god. Please forgive me. I want eternal life, and a loving relationship with You. I believe You that Jesus is the way out of this mess. Please rescue me and change my life now, in Jesus' name. Amen.

If you've prayed a prayer something like this, God is overjoyed, and the Bible says that even the angels in heaven are celebrating because you are so precious to God.

THE FUTURE

We still live on a condemned planet; God has not yet carried out Earth's demolition order, because He wants to keep the door open for more people to come to Him.

The Apostle John saw this vision of what lies ahead:

> Then I saw a new heaven and a new earth, for the first heaven and the first earth had passed away, and there was no longer any sea. I saw the Holy City, the new Jerusalem, coming down out of heaven from God, prepared as a bride beautifully dressed for her husband. And I heard a loud voice from the throne saying, "Look! God's dwelling place is now among the people, and he will dwell with them. They will be his people, and God himself will be with them and be their God. He will wipe every tear from their eyes. There will be no more death or mourning or crying or pain, for the old order of things has passed away."
>
> — REVELATION 21:1–4 (NIV)

This is the future you and I have to look forward to. In the meantime, during the waiting period on this fractured planet there will still be problems in our lives, and we will still make mistakes. Christians still die physically… but not spiritually.

Jesus' death has cleansed you of everything wrong you have ever done, no matter how major or how trivial. He will keep restoring you when you ask forgiveness for every mistake you will make in the future.

The door of your dank, dark cell on death row has swung open. Step into the sunlight, breathe the fresh air of God's love, and move into His plan and purpose for your life. He will be with you through all that lies ahead, in this life and beyond.

WOULD YOU LIKE ANOTHER COPY FOR SOMEONE?

Meet the Real Jesus is available for purchase on all good online bookstores worldwide, as paperback and ebook.

Find bookstore links and further information on the author's website at: https://belindapollard.com/book/meet-the-real-jesus or point your phone camera at this QR code.

A PERSONAL NOTE FROM THE AUTHOR

> **Meet the Real Jesus** was first published as *Closer to God for Newcomers: Meet the Real Jesus* by Scripture Union UK in 2001. Thousands of copies were given out at Soul in the City summer missions in the City of London in the early 2000s.
>
> The book went out of print in 2017 and I intended to republish it, but life was hectic. In 2022, my mother had a significant birthday looming. She was resisting party suggestions, but said, "*I'll* have a party if *you* get that book finished so I can give a copy to guests." I revised and republished it, and she had a party! Thanks for the deadline, Mum. May this book be a blessing.
>
> — BELINDA POLLARD

BULK ORDERS

Meet the Real Jesus is a useful resource or gift for seekers, Alpha course participants, baptism or confirmation candidates, graduating students, chaplaincy clients and others.

| Sample custom covers and custom page insert.

Because of the way we are printing this book, **cover customisation** options are available for orders of 150 or more – for example, add a school crest with colors adjusted to complement, or perhaps a camouflage version for military chaplains.

A **custom page** can also be inserted before the title page for orders of 50 or more – for example, church information or an inspirational short letter addressing graduates or guests.

Order direct from the publisher at **ask@smallbluedog.com** to receive discounts for as few as 10 copies, and to enquire about customisation options.

ABOUT THE AUTHOR

Belinda Pollard is an award-winning Australian mystery author, speaker and former journalist. An accredited book editor and writing coach of twenty years' experience, she co-hosts the Gracewriters Podcast for Christian writers.  She has degrees in Communication (Queensland University of Technology) and Theology (Moore Theological College), and writes the Wild Crimes mystery-thriller series, humorous memoir, Bible meditations, and resources for writers. Her writing prizes include a Varuna Fellowship. Belinda lives in subtropical Brisbane, Australia, where she walks a boisterous small dog and complains about the heat.

belindapollard.com
gracewriters.com
smallbluedog.com

ALSO BY BELINDA POLLARD

COMING SOON
MINI PRAYER JOURNALS
The Landscape of Prayer

Bible Insights on Coping with Trauma

Christmas According to Luke

AVAILABLE NOW IN EBOOK AND PAPERBACK
LIGHT MEMOIR
Dogged Optimism: Lessons in Joy from a Disaster Prone Dog

FICTION
Toxic Delusion: Wild Crimes Prequel

Poison Bay: Wild Crimes Mysteries #1

Venom Reef: Wild Crimes Mysteries #2

WRITING RESOURCES
Use the Power of Feedback to Write a Better Book

www.ingramcontent.com/pod-product-compliance
Lightning Source LLC
Chambersburg PA
CBHW050316010526
44107CB00055B/2259